# THE ART OF THE INTUITIVE HEALER

## VOLUME 1

## WAYNE LEE

Published by:
The moral rights of the author have been asserted.

A catalogue record of this book is available from the British Library.
ISBN 978-1-9999630-2-6

Editor: Angela Clarence
Typesetting/Book Design: Rising Sign Books
Cover design: Marc Thortnon at Digital Shift

# TABLE OF CONTENTS

# INTRODUCTION

Hello and thank you for choosing to pick up this book. I hope this book gets you thinking about, or confirming things for yourself in, your life.

I still believe that I am the person who is most amazed by the outcome of one of my healing sessions! It amuses and bemuses me how I am able to know so much about a client by just the way they walk or the way they lie on the healing couch. It dazzles me that just by knowing a client's age and their siblings ages I can also predict many personality traits and trauma that could come from that family's dynamics. I am the one shocked when I am chatting to a client's inner child as if they are actually there with me. It baffles me when a client is not forthcoming with information yet I can accurately explain, through how they feel to me, what is going on for them.

The reason these skills amaze me is because I have had no official training and grew up totally sceptical and ignorant to this world of spirituality and healing. I have simply developed my many skills or gifts over working with thousands of clients and I am constantly evolving my abilities by being open, intuitive and inspirational during every session. Through the years of my career I have found that marketing in papers and magazines or even specific cate-gory-related media has helped very little. I get 100% of my clientele through word of mouth and by demonstrations of my work for spiritually focused groups.

People will come to me because they are drawn to me. I have had a person walk into one of my demonstrations not knowing at all why she had decided to seek out a spiritual group or talk that day. Having never done so before she was a little confused when she first arrived. Later that night, after my demonstration and before I had even got halfway home, I had received two emails, one call and a text message from her telling me that she was 100% certain she needed to see me and over the following months I saw her, her daughter and her partner for several sessions with much success.

Allowing my clients to find me is important and not wor-rying about it is just as important. The really nice part about being found by word of mouth (or organically) is that it allows for the healing to be far more powerful as the con-nection is natural and "meant to be". It also means that people are speaking positively about my abilities.

I believe that not only am I meant to help others, but that it is my purpose in this life to help them. My agree-ment with my spirit guides and the Universe is such that if my guides ask me to help someone or do something for a spiritual or healing reason based on their, and my, highest of good, I will do it with no questions asked. In return I get a few things I require: health, wealth, harmony, self-growth and thereby the ability to look after my children. I feel this contract with my guides works well and creates the energetic space for clients to find me, employ me and allow me to help them with their healing for the highest of good, even when it is beyond my understanding.

The following stories are of true clients who have willingly given me permission to write about their cases. Some are brief one session cases, some last over years, but each will give you an idea of how healing can be far more than we believe it can be. As I describe each client and case to you I will also explain how I have come to these realisations as best I can.

I am an intuitive healer and I work from the heart. There is no "proof" of the outcome of any of these cases other than the fact that, with my gifts, my integrity and my dignity, I have helped each of these clients to grow and change.

I see no reason to prove anything. I live this life. It is all real to me, even if, often, I am skeptical too.

When I work I do not take responsibility for my clients. I have learned that it is important for me not to worry if my client gets healing or not from my session. I cannot be responsible for my clients healing process in any way or form. All I can do is my very best, while we are in session, to help them with their personal healing process.

I never trust what a client tells me. A client can tell me something that is not true *per se*. They may see it one way (and it is true for them) but that does not mean it is what is actually happening for them. Also a client may withhold sensitive information.

*I helped a client in the past. Her reason for seeing me was because she was struggling with her job and relationships. She was finding it difficult to trust men. I asked many questions waiting for an energetic response and did not get one. After a while I told her either she had forgotten to tell me something important or she was withholding information from me and without that knowledge I could not help her breakthrough and move forward.*

*She sighed and confided in me about a terrible situation that happened with her first boyfriend when she was 18 years old. It had destroyed her trust in men but was so big she was even afraid to talk about it or think about it. I gently worked on it and by the end of the session she was able to confront her own fears over it, without it upsetting her anymore and thus opened up a space for her to be strong enough to allow men back into her life.*

My job is to hold a space. To offer energetic exchange that will unblock energy blockages and shift chakras and create more balance in my client's body. I believe holding a space for a client is more important than anything else a healer can do for their client.

When I say holding a space, it really does not matter what the healing space is like. No amount of decoration or expensive couches or crystals can help to make the space right. The space is about intention, attitude and self-awareness.

The space is about acceptance, compassion, non-judgement and love. Expensive wall paper, matching towels, soft lights and music do not count. I can hold a space in front of 300 people or in a busy, bustling hall at a psychic fayre. I can hold a space in a tent on a field in the middle of nowhere or on the London Underground in peak rush hour whilst speeding along between stations. I can hold a space 30 seconds after having an angry row with my partner. Holding a space is the acceptance of me and my client.

My clients are perfect to me, even riddled with disease or sadness, stuck in a rut or lost in their lives, they are perfect. The last thing they need is someone to brutally judge them or wrong them. That does not help anyone. What they need is someone to see how and why the patterns are there, to be aware of their hurts and sadness and to understand that those good and not so good parts of them make them who they are and are just as important as each other.

Perfection is over rated. True perfection comes from accepting the imperfections that life realistically is. Even a hurting muscle is perfect. A hurting muscle or joint is trying to communicate with the person's conscious mind. So many of us are far too blind to the subconscious, never mind the many cries for assistance that it may be offering us. Even a hurt muscle incurred whilst playing sport can be a message. Why was that muscle weak in the first place?

I believe that we are firstly energetics and then physical. Soul body comes first and physical body second. We are a soul with a body. We are not a body with a soul. What this does for me is allow me to look beyond just the normal healing on a sore knee for instance. I will look at the energetics of that part of the body. I will look and see what is underlying the physical and seek the energetic issue and allow the body then to heal itself through releasing the vibration that is blocking the body's ability to detect the pain or issue. Sometimes it is just purely energetics.

*I was at a local charity function some years ago and I was approached by a gentleman who asked if I was the healer, Wayne. I confirmed I was. He told me he has been suffering from a lower back pain problem for many years and wondered if I could help? I agreed and took a look at his back there and then. Energetically, I could see a break in a meridian energy flow around where his back was hurting him. I thought he must have injured this and my guide told me it was about 20 years ago that it had happened. I asked him what happen to his back 20 years ago.*

*He thought for a moment and told me he had fallen and hurt his back 20 years ago but never thought the two were related.*

*I pulled on the lower energy meridian and intentionally pushed it to reconnect it to the meridian higher up. I told him when he fell, the jolt or injury had broken a meridian flow and the body could not heal what it could not connect to. He had an immediate release of pain and to this day whenever I see him around and about he gives me the thumbs up for it has not hurt him since.*

His pain held a purely energetic reason. It was not due to an emotional trauma but more an outcome of an event that left the energy broken.

Each and every client is unique. I cannot use the same approach with each client as that would be far too limiting. I have to be open, open to any and every possibility. I think the following client case stories will explain this in far more detail.

# ABOUT ME

I am a self-trained intuitive healer. From 29 years of age I consciously started the journey into understanding healing and my personal healing abilities. I have been through the stages of having a huge ego in healing to not believing in myself as a healer at all. I have been through all the internal struggles with being allowed to be the powerful healer or not. I have found myself competing with other healers about who is best, and then also comparing myself to every other healer. I have been through the ups and downs of self-growth and the eye popping realisation that I will have to be working on myself forever! I have to take responsibility for myself (for everything) for the rest of my life and from the moment I was conceived.

This journey has taken me to the point where I am in a place of harmony, where I can be sad and happy at the same time which, I believe, allows me to be a more refined and sensitive healer.

My first memory of connecting to spirit is at the age of 18 months, sitting in a nappy on the cool floor of the kitchen in my home on a scorching day in Johannesburg, South Africa. I recall feeling completely apart from my family and a distinct feeling of sadness and of being unwelcome. I remember the hurt and disconnection which caused me to retreat into myself and into my energy and there, deep inside me, I found a different family, another kind of connection, a connection to my guides and what I now call my spirit family.

I remember my guides always telling me not to tell that they were there with me, not to tell my parents. I recall knowing information and not being able to tell anyone. I think it made me feel more disconnected from my family but more connected to my spirit family. This, I believe, has made it very difficult to remember much about my childhood. I believe I spent most of it connected to my guides rather than reality. It was safer there!

In my 18th year I was standing chopping vegetables, while working as a chef in the 5 star Carlton Hotel in Johannesburg, when I saw an image in my mind's eye of my Father standing with his chest wide open and his heart in his hand. He had a large smile on his face. I recall reprimanding myself for seeing such a harsh thought, but also remembering that my dad was smiling. A few hours later when I got home I found only one car outside my house (which was very unusual with my family). My cousin was sitting on the stairs to our front door waiting for me. She told me that my Father was in hospital. He had gone to the doctor in connection with a hernia and they found it was more serious than that and now he was about to undergo a quadruple heart bypass operation. On hearing this scary news about my Father, I immediately connected to my vision earlier that day. I looked at my cousin and without much reaction and said, "That's ok, it will all be fine. **He was smiling!"** I still went through all the fear and worry when he was having the operation but deep inside me I knew he was going to be ok. Dad was home within a week back to his nutty self in no time.

When I was 19, my good friend had an accidental fall while she was at work in a restaurant and was in serious pain with her back. The swelling was extreme and the doctors said that, until the swelling went down, they could not tell if she would be permanently injured or not. They said it would be weeks before her swelling was reduced enough for them to tell accurately. I visited her the Friday night after her accident and found my friend in serious pain, lying on her bed, unable to sleep or move without hurting. I offered to lightly massage her back. She said, 'No way!' That would be way too painful. She just lay there in pain afraid to move and very tired as she had not slept properly in days. I found myself letting my hands rest on her back. I felt a kind of movement through my hands and then extreme pain shooting up my arms. My friend fell, almost instantly, into a deep sleep and I was sitting there staring amazed at my hands that where holding her back pain. I instinctively shook my hands and released the pain, and energy they were holding, from her back. I took note that I must have some kind of healing ability. I also scorned myself as quickly as I noted the healing ability. At 19 I was not very worldly at all and had no idea about healers, psychics and anything metaphysical or "alternative" and I was beyond completely skeptical. To me it just simply did not exist. The following Monday the doctors found my friends swelling had reduced so much that they could see it was just a lightly slipped disc and she was able to resume her normal life shortly after.

It was ten years later that I moved to live in the UK on an ancestral visa. My Brothers both had immigrated to the UK by then and my Mother was planning to return to the UK, the country of her birth shortly too. My best friend, Peter, had been brutally murdered the year before and I had also recently ended a 3 year relationship so I was looking for change.

On coming to London, I had three months' worth of holiday money to tide me over before looking for work. After a week or so I was getting bored and was sitting at the computer wondering what to type into the search engine to find out about "hands on" healing. My brother, Sean, passed by so I asked him what I should put into the search engine. He said, "Don't put anything in. My friend, Neil, is a Reiki Master. Ask him!" I said, "What is Reiki"?

When I spoke to Neil and asked him what Reiki was he just grinned at me and helped me make a booking for a Reiki level 1 Workshop. The workshop was broken up into two days and after the first day I was walking around with my hands wide open and feeling as if I was on a high, as the energy pulsed through me. My hands felt like I was holding a nuclear power station in each hand. A friend told me I looked like I was King Kong on cocaine!

I did Reiki level two shortly after that and then started giving Reiki to everything, everyone and living my life for Reiki. I explored Reiki beyond what the average person would have done. I spent hours speaking to people on the internet, all over the world, about Reiki. Researching and learning, I joined every Reiki share and Reiki healing group I could find and volunteered to give Reiki constantly. I went through a huge amount of ego fluctuations and obsession with Reiki.

Eventually, I realized there was something wrong with the Reiki I had learned. I blamed the way I was taught. I then did Reiki level one and two another two more times. Eventually, I realised it was 'me' who was using Reiki the wrong way and that I needed to grow up and let myself go and allow Reiki to control me. I stopped being so obsessed with being the healer and let life catch me up and I moved on with living my 'human' life and my 'human' job. I got married and my beautiful daughter, Jade, came along. After a while, when my marriage failed, I got divorced and, during the divorce, I had no choice but to give up my work as a chef. I had my daughter every weekend and as a chef I could not find work that did not include weekends. I started to see clients for Reiki and psychic Readings.

Very quickly after this change in my life, I realised I had been forced to move on to my true path. Everything started to speed up. I went to a spiritual development group and met my close friend Viv. She talked me through my first experience of going into trance and before I knew it I was working with going into trance all the time. We started our own trance circle and I became very adept at it. One afternoon I was in deep trance and a man spoke through me. He spoke in a very clear and powerful voice and said that he was my head doctor and that there were many doctors and healers in spirit that would like to work with me and that I needed to start to do spirit surgery. He said I needed to get a healing couch, lay a client down and put my hands on their head and wait. I would know what to do once I have connected.

A week later we put a healing couch up and people from our circle took turns getting on to the couch. I placed my hands on their heads and waited - then I would just allow myself to move. I would allow myself to be influenced by the person's body and my intuition and before I knew it, I had started developing my method of healing. Within a few weeks I was seeing paying clients and getting results.

*My first paying client for spirit surgery was an acquaintance of mine. He lived locally and was struggling with anxiety. His anxiety was that he could not cope with vehicles controlled by someone else.*

*He was afraid to drive or even be too close to the road because someone else was driving cars and buses around him. He was stuck in our area away from his family who lived up north because he could not get on a bus, train or in a car.*

*It had been 10 years of living in this anxiety and he was now even helping other people deal with their anxiety but could not help himself. He was a Reiki client of mine and he was keen to try spiritual surgery. So we went for it!*

*During the first session I found myself stroking the energy from his heart chakra outward on his chest. It felt like I was stretching and releasing his heart chakra. The strokes across his chest were firm but gentle, actually only a light massage at the hardest. The session went on with me doing a variety of things that I did not understand, but knew I needed to do. We finished the session and we booked another session for the following week.*

*Two days later I called him to ask if he had any effect from the healing. He asked me if I had beaten him as he said his chest felt like he had been repetitively punched and he felt like he was severely bruised.*

*We did the next session and I spent most of the session with my hands on his head and also released his heart chakra again. He decided that he would wait and see what the outcome was before booking another session.*

*I called him on his mobile phone a few days later to get some feedback and to see if his chest felt beaten again. He answered and said to me, "Guess what? I am on a bus on the way up north to see my Mum. I am not scared anymore. Thank you".*

The strange thing is that I did not believe that I was helping people. It took me years, and hundreds of clients later, to prove to myself that I was getting these kinds of results, that I was helping people.

I became paranoid to some degree and would not go out shopping during the day because one time I crossed paths with a client of mine in my local superstore and when I noticed her, and was about to wave, she turned towards a person she was with, and while whispering, pointed at me. I became very wary of public places, even more than normal.

In the beginning when I was working with clients, I would be influenced by my guides, higher-self or the clients body to do different things, pull toes, push specific areas, pull on the chakras, use one hand instead of two, move a finger a few millimeters to the left and many more, what seemed back then as peculiar things. Then, although I started to become very accepting of these things, a big part of my mind was sitting there watching my guides control all of this and was getting more and more inquisitive.

I started asking why I was doing this, why I was doing that, what did this mean, what did that mean? The answers would start to come quicker and quicker and the more I asked the more answers I got.

Sometimes it would take months for me to understand things and I would get really excited when I did get it. Through this inquisitive nature, I now have the ability to explain most of what I do or have an understanding of what is happening and sometimes what to expect after a treatment. Of course, this is from my own point of view.

It has taken me years of work seeing clients and working on my own issues to allow me the privilege of having the confidence to write this book. I hope it helps you.

# Rachel in Life and Death

## Overview

In this case study I explain how important it is to "hold a space" for a client. How trusting your intuition and being aware of your surroundings is very important in being an intuitive healer. How life can be taken so easily from us and how we can fight back and survive beyond the odds. It is also a story of death and how accepting our mortality is a life giving power to itself.

Rachel comes to me through intuition and love and together we give her many more years of life against the odds, and when she decides it is time for her to move on, together we make that a possibility for her too. I also explain that being the healer is also being the student.

## Booking

Rachel's booking came through email from one of Rachel's closest and oldest friends, Sophia. Sophia asked if I would go and see Rachel in her own home as Rachel was physically and mentally unwell. Sophia's husband had seen me previously with some success. She had been given my name by her National Health doctor because they could not get any results helping her husband's increasingly worsening irritable bowel syndrome (IBS). In a few sessions we had great success in reversing most of the symptoms of his IBS.

*I am very cautious of taking bookings that are booked on behalf of someone else. However, I also have to trust that we are all intuitive and that often people need a push in the right direction. Sophia proved this to me in this case; she knew instinctively when I was needed; she knew when her dear, lifelong friend needed help, and she acted upon it. This shows how well she is connected to her intuition.*

*IBS is a very common ailment that clients come to see me for. The following is the way I describe this ailment energetically: when there is held trauma or unexpressed emotion in our energy field, our energy will vibrate at a different vibration to our optimal vibration. This change in vibration causes our body to struggle to correspond with itself, so we have uncontrolled change in our body that our mind does not become aware of, and therefore does not deal with. We know, scientifically, that if you put a brick in a vibration for long enough, the brick will eventually corrode from the vibration, breakdown and disintegrate. If your stomach is in an unstable vibration and the body is unable to communicate with it, after years of miscommunication, the body develops differ-ent unusual symptoms: Symptoms perhaps like IBS, Crohn's disease, gallstones, kidney stones, intolerances, al-lergic reactions, endometriosis, etc. What if the trauma is vi-brating uncontrollably around the spine? Then we could get bone degeneration and back pain. Think about the body cells that are in that vibration and how they could be af-fected by the constant, irregular vibration, causing them to replicate into abnormal cells, causing disease.*

*The vibration in our energy body (soul) can affect our physical body. If we release the vibration by dealing with the emotional trauma that caused the vibration, we can change a person's physical body. I have seen the change happen so fast that the client notices it immediately or the change can take a longer time, over several months or even a year, but eventually the client will know there has been change.*

*One of my clients, after her session, was walking around in circles outside by her car. I went down to see if she was ok; she told me that it had been such a long time since she had been able to walk without pain that she was just enjoy-ing the moment.*

*When I first started my healing journey, I worked as a volunteer at a healing group in London where we had a 65-year old gentleman arrive with two walking sticks to aid his movements. He told me he had been using those sticks for 12 years and no doctor could understand what was causing his intense back pain that was almost crippling him. He chose to have a twenty minute healing session with me. We struggled to get him on the bed since he could only lie in one position on a firm healing bed: on his stomach, with several pillows propping up his chest and head. I started the healing and found myself lost in the energetics. Back then I did not understand what I was doing, not as I do now.*

*After fifteen minutes the gentleman said: "You might as well stop now, there is no point in carrying on".*

*At first I was worried he was unhappy with me.*

*I asked him why there was no point in continuing and he said: "a few minutes ago I felt the pain intensify then move from my back down my legs and out my feet and it's gone now. "*

*True to his word, his pain of 12 years had gone. From that day on, this gentleman would be the first to arrive at our Thursday night group to help set up the chairs and beds. I think it was his way of saying 'thank you' for having a group available for healing.*

*Towards the end of my time volunteering at that group he came to me and asked if he could have some healing. A little surprised, I asked him if the pain had come back. He shook his head and said with a huge smile: "NOPE, the*

*Missus had me putting up curtains all day yesterday - back is a bit stiff."*

*Healing can create change immediately and it can be very long lasting. This gentleman had come to terms with his trauma, either through working through it, or accepting himself just as he was. The trauma was no longer actually active in him, so when the healing connected to him, and attempted to re-balance his body, it simply pushed the residue trauma causing the pain to shift out of his body.*

*Other clients may find this takes longer because they have not worked on the trauma or accepted the trauma yet. Some clients will resist healing as much as possible. This is not usually a conscious choice, and our bodies do not like change either. They feel safer in a comfortable, unchanging flow, so sometimes I get clients who have a severe response to the healing; the worst has been getting home and throwing up several times.*

*One of my favourites (responses or stories) was when a lady phoned me at 11pm one evening asking me what she should do. Her husband had come to see me that afternoon at 2pm. When he got home he went to bed and had not woken yet. He slept from 3.30pm all through the night until 8.30am in the morning. Now that's a response to a healing session! Some clients experience the reaction before the session; feeling unstable before they even arrive to see me.*

*There is no way of me knowing what the outcome of each session will be. I do enjoy seeing the changes and hearing the stories though. One of the most common changes I hear from clients is that they notice they behave differently in their normal life situations e.g. "usually I would get angry, but this time I did not" or "usually that would emotionally hurt me, but this time it did not" and "normally I just do it, this time I told them no!"*

## MY PREPARATION

I travelled to see Rachel.

All the information I had was that this client, Rachel, had recently come out of hospital after major surgery to remove cancer and had undergone cancer treatments. I was also seeing Rachel because of her internal struggle with her fears of life and death. My preparation was to embrace calm. No matter what Rachel was going through, she needed me to be able to hold a space and to hear her, to be able to connect to her energetically and allow her to release her fear.

One of my personal issues is time keeping. I do not like being late, so I always leave with plenty time to get somewhere. This is always part of my preparation because I know I must be early to avoid getting stressed out with myself before arriving at a client. The last thing Rachel would need was for me to be stressed when I arrived. I am not a very fussy person, but some things irritate me immensely, and being late is one of them. (Toilet paper the wrong way on the holder is another).

Intuitively, I knew that Rachel was in a total state of anxiety. As I made my way to her, I could feel this anxiety vibrating against my energetics and it made me slightly uncomfortable, but it also gave me insight into how calm I needed to be. I needed to meet her anxiety with an equal amount of openness and calm.

*As I mentioned in previous chapters, holding a space is, I believe, one of the most important factors of offering healing. I believe a large number of healers get confused with the difference between holding a space and making a space. Healers work really hard in making a space that is suitable to assist the healing process. They worry about the colour of the walls in their space, the comfort of the healing couch. They buy top quality blankets, pillows and couch covers (all matching colours of course). They decorate the room in a very specific manner with natural woods and soft lighting, as many crystals as they can squeeze into their room; fragrances, scents and sticks are a must. The right music is essential, with different sounds of the forest and ocean and, of course, Gregorian monks chanting, and bells chiming and ringing. That's it. The room is ready, the space is set. The healer now has a space to see clients in.*

*Again, I think it would shock people that I have given healing on the London underground, in a field, whilst on a train to London, in a night club at 4am in the morning.*

*I have helped people over the phone whilst they are throwing up in another country, on a bus, driving in my car, in the middle of an argument, in a restaurant and standing at the counter of the local takeaway. Holding a space is not about the location, it's about your ability to accept a person and make them feel accepted, so they can be free to be them-selves.*

*Holding a space is creating an open place in your heart and soul that is free of judgment and ridicule, a place where it's okay for the person to be in their fears and traumas, a safe place where they can be vulnerable and will not be at-tacked, no matter what.*

*This space has to be created on a foundation of genuine honesty, with no holding back, even if what is said, heard, felt and expressed may not always be the easiest for the client to hear and may cause a strong emotional response but because the space is safe the client is safe release; a space working for the highest of good of the client.*

*Holding a space is not as simple as many may think. What makes a person good at holding a space is the ability to see their own trauma in that space along with their client's trauma. Often I will be aware that I am beginning to speak to or treat a client in a way that's different from what I would normally feel while holding a space. I take this personal change very seriously, because it is most probably a client's projection on to me, an unseen belief about themselves.*

*The client may have connected their trauma to me and I have accepted that trauma and am now playing it out for them. Whilst I am holding a space, I am also holding myself in this space. I am watching my every word and move and seeing where I may be acting differently. I use this information to help me work with a client.*

*I was with a client in her first session with me. I asked her about her childhood and how she would get punished if her parents had thought she had done something wrong? I wanted to gauge where her childhood beliefs were focused. I wanted to know if she had negative personal beliefs, if she believed she was bad, naughty, wrong or unacceptable.*

*As she spoke, I found myself thinking about something totally random and not connected to her at all. I noticed her talking away whilst I was not listening to her. I asked her to stop talking. I allowed the energy she was projecting on me to enter into my energy even more; I welcomed it. I listened to it and it spoke to me, it gave me a structural understanding of this part of her that was projecting the belief that she was 'not worthy of being heard'.*

*I asked her if she ever got her way as a child, if her parents or family ever really listened to her.*

*She thought for a moment and then said: "No, there were strict rules to adhere to, there was no-one listening, kids just did what they were told". We immediately got on the healing bed and released her beliefs attached to her being heard and her self-worth.*

*Whilst I am holding a space, I am also watching myself, so that I can be aware of how I am reacting in relation to the client. I think I repeat this point over and over in this book and also when I am teaching and running workshops, but everything that happens in a healing session is relevant. If a fly flies passed by, it is relevant. It's just up to us to work out what the relevance is.*

*How often do we get a chance to be accepted exactly as we are? This, I believe, is actually the job of our mothers and fathers. Unfortunately, society has taken this natural parenting out of the way we raise and consider our children and, as a replacement, we have tremendous expectations of our children even before they are born, who will therefore never be acceptable because they must live up to expectations that are not their own. I see clients easily healing their personal issues because I am holding a space for them; a space where I do not wrong them, think they are bad or naughty. I do not have expectations of them and I do not project my personal needs onto them.*

*Think about it, how often have you actually been somewhere where you feel totally accepted? If you have, you will remember feeling very special; it will have been an important event for you.*

*This is why my clients remember their sessions in such detail and hence why I have learned not to reveal all the work I am doing on a client, to that client. I have learned that revealing too much gives clients the opportunity to spend hours analysing and scrutinising something that needs to be out of their body and their attention to it could reinstall it back into the body, recreating the same issues within themselves.*

## ARRIVAL

I was warmly greeted by Rachel and her daughter. Instantly, I was aware of my body vibration changing. The increased erratic vibration was intense and uncomfortable for me; this was clearly the shock and anxiety that Rachel's body was in. I immediately knew that she had not yet recovered from the shock her body had experienced from being operated on. This would be a key factor for me to work on.

The trauma a body goes through during a major operation, that also has such huge fear of life and death attached to it, can cause an immense unbalancing such that the body and mind will find it hard to calm itself and be able to be on a reasonable level of consciousness and rational thought.

I was welcomed into Rachel's home. Rachel was happy to have her daughter in the room with us. I was mindful that I needed to hold a space for her daughter just as much as I did for Rachel.

As I was focusing on Rachel, I was also aware that her daughter must have also gone through trauma with her mother's cancer and the fear of losing her mum.

I was also acutely aware of her daughters energetics being that of complete interest in what I was doing and if I was going to help her mum, but it felt as if she was creating a wedge of energy in my connection with Rachel, so I created a separate space to hold her daughter - a warm but very clinical space to keep her energetics at bay so they could no longer affect my awareness of her mother.

*I do not find it a problem to have other people in the room when I am working. I have demonstrated my work in front of 250 people before and find it very exhilarating and, subsequently, tiring. I have to hold a space and energetics for all those people watching, as well as the person I am working on at that exact point in time.*

*Although, if I find a client is not being open with me during their session and they have a partner, parent or friend with them, I will ask the other person to move out of the room for the rest of the session so that the client is able to be open without fear of hurting these other people. However, this in itself is a very important message for me to consider, as I am then aware that the client has a belief that they are not allowed to be themselves, or that they feel responsible for other people's emotions. Everything is relevant.*

*A young lady came to see me. In her first two sessions her mum came along for moral support and seemed to be very open in the sessions. However, when the young lady came for her third session, she was alone. It was like chalk and cheese.*

*The first two sessions I was working with a girl, but in the third session, the woman had arrived. I pointed out how much her energy changed around her mum, and asked her if she realised that she was changing into a childlike energy when her mum was around.*

*She said she was aware that she felt like she was losing her power when she was with her mum. She shared with me that more often than not she feels controlled, belittled and irritated when she was with her mum.*

*I explained that this feeling would have been created as a little girl trying to make her mum happy by being good and by seeking confirmation that she was behaving in a manner that her parents would have been happy with. This pattern has worked well to keep her safe as a little girl but as an adult it is now no longer relevant, but is still active and it is now her responsibility as a grown women to re-educate that little girl energy within her to not react in the same way.*

*She has found herself now resentful of the way her mum behaves around her. When we feel resentful it is because we are not looking at our own needs and taking responsibility for them. Instead we are blaming someone else for them, and in return offering them our power.*

*I do not believe it is possible for someone to take our power away. I often have clients tell me their mother or partner or ex-partner is an energy leach or vampire. I do not believe this to be possible.*

*I believe these people are just triggering our fears and we are feeding them our energy out of an uncontrolled trauma response.*

*When we can see this, and take responsibility for this trauma, and work on the trigger, then we release the trauma and will no longer respond to it in the usual way.*

*Once we learn the skills of how to take responsibility for ourselves, it gets easier and easier and we become more and more able to hold our own power.*

## Skill

If someone in your life is constantly triggering you into giving them your energy, time and power, it can be difficult to stop this process. This is a skill I teach many of my clients to help them start to change this personal behaviour pattern.

*Most of us will know when we are being triggered to give our power away. The connection between us and the person who is triggering us will trigger feelings of being in trouble, we feel nervous or tired, drained, scared or even a physical gut twisting or stomach wrenching feeling.*

*When this happens you start by internally speaking to that person who is triggering you. You say in your mind to them "Thank you, but you cannot have my power".*

*Some more examples are:*

- *Thank you for calling me **but you cannot have my power.***
- *Thank you for coming over **but you cannot have my power.***
- *Thank you for your text **but you cannot have my power.***
- *Thank you for your suggestion **but you cannot have my power.***
- *Thank you for thinking you know what is best for me **but you cannot have my power.***

*When I do this, I think of putting my hand up in front of me as I say, **"but you cannot have my power."** And I make sure that I say it with a guttural effort. We always say 'thank you' no matter how awful or manipulative the interaction is because it is always good to be open to connection, but we can then choose to close the door to that connection. If we use aggressive, hateful and pushy thoughts or words toward the person who is triggering us, we are then feeding them our energy. When we say 'thank you', we are open and freely willing to accept their energetic approach and then giving ourselves time to decide if we wish to give a response or to close the door.*

*The reason this begins to work quickly is that it causes us to become aware of our behaviour so we can see when we are actually giving our power away. This teaches us about our own processes and gives us the skills to change who we are deep down inside. It will help us to see what we need to work on to make those needed changes within. We must all always remember that everything that happens to us is our own responsibility.*

*To explain this further, if someone is texting us and the messages are triggering us, through their attacking words or manipulative manner, we need to take responsibility for ourselves and not blame the person sending us the message.*

*We must look at why they feel they can do this and change this within ourselves. Because we become aware of how we are dealing with our power we then learn to control it and thus take responsibility for our true needs.*

*This will also stop people from doing this to us in the future. An example is if your parents would punish you when they thought you were naughty and from this, you developed a belief that you deserve to be punished. If this is so, on an energetic level, you begin telling people to punish you because you have learned through your parents that it is ok for you to be punished.*

*As a child you had no choice and hence hold the belief*

*that you deserve to be punished. As an adult it becomes our responsibility to decide to tackle the beliefs of our childhood and re-educate ourselves to behave in the way we as adults believe we should behave in accordance to our personal life's choices and concepts.*

## BASIC INFO

Rachel is in her 60's. She is a mother of three with two grandchildren. She seems frail for her age and thinner than seems natural. She seems uncertain in herself. She is of African decent and has a distinct African accent. Rachel has been on antidepressants and sleeping pills for more years than she can remember.

*My belief about anti-depressants is that they can be helpful in short, controlled doses, but in longer term use they mask the true problem a person is having and allow the person to hide from their own issues.*

*Hidden or masked trauma becomes distressed in the body. Distressed trauma gradually becomes a stronger energetic vibration in the body that can eventually become diseased.*

*Disease is far more difficult to deal with as the energetic vibration has compounded itself into the physical body. It has manifested itself in the body so the person has to see it and deal with it. However, we seem to only use physical methods to deal with dis-ease when it occurs and ignore the emotional factors creating a recurring issue.*

*I believe everything is energetic first and physical second. Deal with the energy and the physical will heal. Deal with only the physical and the energetic will recreate the same issue until it is dealt with energetically.*

*Trauma is simply the body's way of saying 'help me, look at me, I am unbalanced, explain things to me, give me your attention and please hear me'.*

*When depression is a factor it means that we are not in touch with our emotional body. We are not in touch with our own needs and then we take anti-depressants and become even more detached from ourselves and now with the aid of the drugs in anti-depressants we cannot even hear the body trying to communicate with us. Anti-depressants are a way out of dealing with your own emotional situation; a cop-out of taking responsibility for ourselves.*

*With all the clients I have worked with that have depression, one thing I have seen come clearly through is that almost none of my clients actually know what depression is, they have not even looked it up in a dictionary. When I ask them to define depression they always offer me a list of symptoms of depression. For instance, depression is always feeling down, not being able to cope with situations, being sad, being overwhelmed. All these are not an explanation of depression, but rather the way they are feeling whilst they are depressed.*

*I believe depression is an accumulation of overwhelming, undealt with emotions and trauma. I believe that the way that most of us are taught to deal with our emotions in our childhood makes us believe that being emotional is bad and wrong.*

*We get told: "crying is for babies". We hear: "I'll give you something to cry about", "big boys and girls don't cry", "do not shout at me", etcetera. We get taught to ignore our emotions, all but happiness, which we are taught is worthy, but that the rest of our emotions are bad.*

*I believe depressed people have not been taught how to express their emotions properly and thus hold them energetically in their energy field and their body cannot cope with that extreme emotional vibration and it thus overwhelms the person's emotional state, creating a sense of not being able to cope with day-to-day life.*

*Our upbringing and society have taught us that being emotional is bad and have inevitably created depression. Truly dealing with depression is ultimately the goal of self-*

*acceptance. Dealing with depression is not an easy process. Once you start you can never turn back and the ending is only at the end of our lives. This must sound extremely overwhelming for someone with depression. Yes, it's hard, but it's so very worthwhile. Yes, it's long, but it gets easier as you learn the skills to deal with it and life becomes so much more rewarding. Everyone could learn to connect to him or herself better than they already do.*

*The way I would suggest dealing with depression is learning the skills that help us take responsibility for our own actions.*

**Skill one**: *Knowing when to take responsibility.*

*If you are blaming someone for something it's because you are not taking responsibility for it yourself. This rule counts always!! No matter what!! You must always take responsibility for yourself. (This is called growing up).*

**Skill two**: *See your part in everything.*

*No matter what happens in any connection with anyone, always look to see why you have created this for yourself. Ask yourself:" what have I done to create this?"" did I cause this?"" what could I have done differently to change this situation?"*

*For instance, if two people are having an argument, it's because they cannot see eye to eye on a situation; hence the argument. What is really happening is that each person is arguing with themselves because they are unwilling to take responsibility for either being wrong or not willing to accept that someone else is right or wrong or they do not want to change their point of view. "You are wrong, I am right" is the inner argument, so the argument is internal and being projected at the other person. This refers back to skill one - if you are blaming you are not taking responsibility for yourself.*

**Skill three**: *Be genuine*

*If you are sad, be sad. If you are angry, be angry. If you are happy, be happy. Try not to take your emotional situation out on others, but if you do, apologise for taking it out on them.*

*Do not apologise for being emotional. **You are allowed to be emotional**. In the beginning this can be hard but, as time goes by, you learn to allow your emotions to flow and it gets easier and easier and you learn to accept yourself more.*

**Skill four**: *Be nice to yourself.*

*No matter what is happening for you in your life, realise*

*that you are a creation of your past and that most of it was out of your control and due to society and childhood influences, so stop blaming yourself for everything, and start to be compassionate towards yourself.*

*Give yourself a break. You are worth it. The most amazing thing happens when you are nice to yourself... you start being nicer to others too. And people start being nicer to you.*

**Skill five**: *Self-parenting work*

*Learn to do inner child work and re-teach yourself how to behave in your life.*

*Inner child work is a well-known therapeutic method of connecting with the childhood parts of yourself that are in trauma and releasing them from their trauma by acknowledging them with compassion and love. Accepting them just as they are, by being aware of how each part of you is feeling and then re-educating them so they can learn to be free from their traumas.*

**Skill six**: *Welcome the lessons*

*Expect and accept that you will be wrong many times in your life. When you are wrong do not beat yourself up for it. Just see it as a way of learning about yourself and try and get it right next time.*

*We learn through our childhood, schooling and friends that being wrong is bad, we become afraid of being wrong and end up beating ourselves up for it, or pushing ourselves beyond what is needed to be right, or commonly (with depression) not trying anything just in case we are wrong.*

*As human beings, it is in our nature to get it wrong and learn from it. If it was not, none of us would be walking or talking. It took Thomas Edison thousands of wrongs to get it right. He said he learned thousands of ways of how 'not' to make a light bulb. He never gave up, and without him our lives would not be the same. Welcome the errors; learn from them. When life throws you a curve ball and you miss, giggle at it, and then get ready to try hitting the next curve ball life throws at you.*

**Skill seven***: Remember you are human.*

*Be at least 51% human all the time. The other 49% can be spiritual or religious or depressed. Give yourself a break, don't beat yourself up.*

*You are a flawed human: accept it. It's not supposed to be easy, so you might as well join in and enjoy the ride.*

*The perfection of humanity is the acceptance of our imperfections. Nothing on earth is actually perfect if you look closely enough. But there is perfection in the earth's natural, organic, genuine state if we accept it just the way it is. The path to total acceptance can only lead to genuine organic love.*

*Some years ago, just after I got divorced, I had my daughter temporarily taken away, I had my step-son permanently taken away, I lost my job and had lost all my passion for life and I was very close to my personal end. I sat in my bedroom seriously contemplating suicide. I sat asking my guides what I should do about my life. They made me realise that if I did kill myself, the world would continue without me and everything would be back to normal in most people's lives very quickly. My daughter and family may get hurt but they would survive like others have done in the history of our planet.*

*The conclusion I came to was that there was no point in killing myself. It would not benefit anyone, it would not prove anything, and it would most definitely not benefit me. So I decided to live and just be me. I decided to take chances and go for it. I decided that the worst that could happen was death and death was inevitable anyway, so I learned to just go for it in life. I accepted my humanity and that I was going to make mistakes, and the mistakes would help me learn how to be a better human being.*

*No matter what I am doing, no matter how close to my guides, spirit surgeons I get, no matter how clearly I can sense and see energy, I am still always human - so I need to keep that part real. I need to be human and expect to mess up all the time. It's what I, as a human being, am supposed to do: learn from my mistakes.*

**Skill eight:** *Accept everyone just as they are.*

*When you start to accept people as they are, with all their flaws and irritating habits, you begin to allow acceptance into your life. Accept everyone and you will accept yourself. Make new friends even if you do not usually like 'those kinds' of people. Allow people in your life; allow life into your life.*

## REASON FOR SEEING ME

Rachel has just been through serious operations for cancer and is suffering from fear and anxiety. She is also having difficulty with her eyesight since the discovery of cancer and her hearing is deteriorating.

*Through the years of seeing clients with cancer I have come to the understanding that if a client with any issue is drawn to see me through a gut feeling, an unexplainable knowing that I can help them, then I will be able to help them. How I will help them I do not know and will never know for sure, but if they come to me from the right place within themselves then they have been drawn to me and have chosen to allow me to help them with their healing, and thus they have already created the change needed in themselves. But, if a person chooses to see me because they have heard I have helped other people with their healing process, and they want me to help them through their need to be rescued, I will not be able to help them. I cannot rescue anyone. I do not believe I can heal anyone, I believe I can help people on their healing journey.*

*I can help balance out energy, I can help remove energetic blockages, I can help explain an energetic situation in the body or between people, but I cannot do the healing for the client.*

*It's all up to each of us to heal ourselves, but we all need help in the healing process somewhere along the way. It is my calling, my life path to help people. I can't help everyone, but if a client is drawn to me, I know without a single bit of doubt in my mind that I will be able to help them. How I will help them, I do not even want to ponder. Sometimes it will be clear, sometimes it will be revealed later, and sometimes we will never know. But the healing help will be there. This is why my personal work ethic is that I offer: "Healing for the highest of good beyond my understanding with total integrity."*

*I had a client book in to see me and the night before seeing me he started being sick, throwing up more than he has ever done before, without feeling ill or being under the weather in any way at all. He contacted me to cancel his session. I told him that because he had chosen to come and see me the energetic movement within him would have already started to shift.*

*I suggested that he come and see me if he could as it would be far more beneficial for his healing process. Obviously if he was still very poorly we would re-schedule. He did come and see me and the healing session was one of those that left me smiling. I knew the energy shifted very strongly and I knew his life had changed. He commented on it too. He commented on how he immediately felt different; he felt different because he chose to heal.*

*Not all clients get a reaction as strong and as quickly as that. Some clients see the changes in themselves over months.*

*One client called me 6 weeks after her session to tell me that she noticed that, in certain situations in her life, she had started to behave with more confidence. Before, she would submit to other people's needs; but since her 2 sessions with me she had realised that she could now define what is right or wrong for her and was now able to hold her power in any situation.*

*I cannot explain what will happen in a healing session or after the healing session, but I have no doubt that there will be some sort of change for the client. I know this because every session I participate in, changes me.*

## THE SESSION

I talked to Rachel about her body being in shock. I told her she had not only been through the trauma of finding out she had cancer, but also the trauma of going through a life-saving operation that had her facing the huge fears of whether she was going to live or die.

I explained to her that her body and mind were probably so totally overwhelmed with all of this that it was impossible for her to make any sense of life or death at that point. Rachel told me that she had had trauma all the way through her life and that she found it very difficult to show her emotions. Rachel also asked me if I would work on her hearing and her eyesight. She said that she was finding it hard to read and reading was very important to her. Reading was her escape and had been since her childhood.

I was aware that for Rachel to have had such serious cancer she must be holding extreme trauma. I could see no reason at that point to work on that trauma. We had to first and foremost sort out her anxiety and fears, and balance her body and energy. I know that fear, anxiety and stress create an acidic reaction in the body and acidic bodies are prone to disease.

*Not every client needs the same things; each client is unique. I wait for each client to tell me what they need from me. I do this by holding my energetic field as close to my body as I can. I pull all my attention into me, I ground and connect to myself and hold myself in my body with total acceptance. This process usually also opens my chakras allowing me to connect even more clearly with my guides and gets my intuition really sparking. It also allows me to be extra sensitive towards my client's energetics. Then I wait. I wait for my client's energy to reach me and to vibrate against my own energetics.*

*I have spent years and years working on my own energy, on getting to know my own energetic feeling, learning how my energy feels in me, around me and through me, so I know which vibration is mine and which vibration is that of a client. I listen to these vibrations against my body and am alert to their position and how they make me feel. I allow them to create ideas in my mind and I am not afraid of re-telling these to my client.*

*I am not afraid of getting it wrong, and I do, often. A client will say: "no, that's not right for me." I welcome being wrong*

*- it shows me how to be right in the future. Lately however, I seem to be wrong less often. I am right most of the time, from my own point of view.*

*Clients may not understand it exactly as I explain it and sometimes I cannot even explain it. It's just a concept, a vibration, a frequency or all three mixed together creating an idea, a picture, and then I leave it up to my intuition to work out how to process this idea into a healing solution for my client. I allow the client's energy to lead me through to what is happening for them and I trust myself, I accept myself, and I accept and trust the feeling from them.*

*The most amazing part of this is that as I accept and trust my client, so they automatically receive healing from me.*

*If we could all learn to truly accept ourselves, we would automatically also learn to accept everyone else, and vice versa, then our world would be a much healthier place.*

## ON THE HEALING BED

The first time Rachel got on the bed, all my usual insights were not used. I did not worry about her body position; I did not worry about her hand positions. There was no point working out the past traumas and energetics and changing them on someone who was in immediate shock and trauma. *See part 1*

My first connection with Rachel was on her shoulders, a classic healing position to help release stress, shock and trauma. I placed my left hand on her left shoulder and my right hand on her right shoulder making sure I was on the soft tissue between the neck and shoulder bones. I held this position allowing my energetics to connect completely with Rachel. After several minutes and a defined calming of her energy, a few uncontrollable deep breaths were released from Rachel and me and I was ready to move to her abdomen. I moved to her abdomen, where what happened thereafter was a real first for me. *See part 2*

I placed my hands over her stomach, just allowing them to lie there randomly; allowing the connection to be confirmed and deepened. I began to go into a semi-trance state.

As I allowed my vision to become shallower, or less focused on her body, I started to see past her skin as if it were invisible. I could see cells and energy movements; I could also see sparkly, glittery type cells that felt very wrong to me. These cells screamed disease to me but to this day I am not sure what they actually were. All I knew was that if I pinched into her body energetically I could release them from her body.

To this day I am not sure whether I was removing diseased cells or traces of the chemicals left in Rachel's body from her treatment. I spend a long time scanning into her body looking for more of these glittery cells. I was just about to make my way back to her shoulder to check how her level of shock was doing, and to work on her hearing and eyesight, when I noticed in her abdomen (just above the sacral chakra) that there was something curled up like a spiral. This was something I had also never seen before. I was interested to know what this was curled up in her abdomen.

As usual with my guides, I asked the questions but did not expect an immediate answer, but this time I received an answer instantly: this is nothing you can work on, it's not a problem for Rachel and it would be removed easily and reasonably soon. I told Rachel about this spiral in her stomach and that it was not something I could remove, but somehow it would be removed shortly, and it would not be a problem. I told her perhaps it was something that needed to be done further down the line, when she was more balanced. About this, truthfully I had no understanding and was just guessing, but I have 100% faith in my guides and knew it would show itself when it was ready. *See part 3*

I moved up to Rachel's eyes, I asked her how long her eyesight had been this bad and she said since she found out about her illness it had deteriorated.

I held the energy around her eyes; I allowed my thumbs to rest on her closed eye lids so I could connect with her eye ball very gently. I received an image of Rachel being so uncertain of the future that she could not see the future and this energetic was slowly getting stronger, fuelled by her fear of death and leaving her family. Rachel was slowly allowing fear to blind her. I worked the energy around her eyes over and over again, releasing as much of the thick and syrupy energy as I could grasp. I could feel my guides creating energetic tubes or drains. They have done this many times before, placing energy drains into the energetic around the eye allowing the energy to be drained away until it is no longer causing an effect. I thought it would be interesting to see the outcome of this energy clearing in the future. *See part 4*

I moved to Rachel's ears and became immediately aware of a similar energetic about 'being heard', around her ears. It gave me images of Rachel's childhood that revealed that she was not well looked after and that her needs were not met.

Rachel did not expect to be heard. I was aware that this energetic belief was considerably deeper than that around her eyes and every attempt I made to clear the energetic was blocked by her beliefs about herself that were so deep that I realised it would take a good few sessions focusing on this mistaken belief to make a shift in her hearing. *See part 4*

I checked on Rachel's energy again, making sure it was balanced, and felt it was far more vibrant and moved more smoothly than before. She had spent over 60 minutes on the bed, which is much longer than I would normally offer someone in shock, as this could also unsettle them. I asked Rachel to sit up and assess how she was feeling. *See part 5*

I spent the rest of the session gently discussing my beliefs about death and life with Rachel and her daughter, giving them something to think about as an alternative to the beliefs they have adopted from the normal societal beliefs about death. *See part 6*

As I was about to leave, Rachel asked me: "Wayne, please can you tell me, am I dying?" I answered: "Rachel, just like all the other humans on earth, you are dying, but I think you will have to wait a while longer just like the rest of us!" I have seen death before, and this did not seem like death to me. *See part 7*

Rachel felt very clear and clean to me after the session, her smile was larger and her energy was no longer in such extreme shock. They agreed to come and see me at my home and healing room a few weeks later so that I could assist in furthering and maintaining Rachel's balance. *See part 8*

## PART 1

*When I am working with a client in shock I once again make the connection to the client with total acceptance. I am allowing their body to have a connection that will soothe the body almost as a mother would soothe a child. The ability to accept that the client is in this state and to hold the energetics for them is a very important tool to allow the client to release the stress and trauma of shock.*

*Their body is overwhelmed and holding this space for them creates an opening to allow the shock to release. I am also very aware of the process and will have a few deep breaths of release as the shock starts to release.*

*I want to explain what I mean by accepting others as perfect, from my point of view. I always see the good in people. I am willing to accept that I am wrong and that I might be seeing things incorrectly. I have learned to judge people in an open way. I judge them with my gut instinct and then wait to see if I am right or wrong. Sometimes I am pleasantly surprised because someone is far more open then I have judged them to be. Sometimes I am surprised that people can be so very closed. Yet because I judge openly I am not projecting my own beliefs on to them.*

*When we judge in a closed way, we are projecting our total belief on a person and thus we are creating in them our judgment. This is something that I believe is crippling our world: we judge people for their colour, stature in life, nationality, age, sex and in so many more ways, each of which prevents us from allowing the connection of energy. Judgements that are closed lock the door to connection with that person, or that segment of people, and thus create disconnection and disharmony, within us, as well as the people we project onto.*

*An open judgment to a client comes from a point of offering acceptance; a closed judgment to a client will compound their fears and traumas and not allow them to heal.*

*With my clients, I am open to anything. I allow my judgements to be extremely fine and totally open and allow my clients to teach me what I need to know about their bodies and how I need to help them.*

*Some clients just need to have hands on their shoulders to start the process of healing. Some clients just need to book a session for the healing to begin powerfully. The choice to see a healer is a powerful healing tool.*

## PART 2

I believe the most common known healing techniques for healers is that of placing hands on to people's shoulders (other than a cuddle). It is a position I use often too, but it useful to also be aware of how this works.

The hands on shoulders is creating an energy boost into the client that increases energy flow and suggests to the client a left-right or male-female energetic balancing.

Think of it as a flat battery of a car that you are wiring up; you put positive to positive and negative to negative. So in the same way you place right hand onto right shoulder, left hand onto left shoulder and you boost the client's energy streaming through their body.

This boost of energy clears loose or stubborn energy blocks and re-charges a client's energy which is always good. I do believe this works, but if this is the only technique that a healer is using, then the client should expect to need months and years of healing. I do not believe just a boost of energy is enough to create a deep clearing from a client's lifelong trauma. The clients who would get a huge release from this would have already done the release of energy through either therapy, other forms of healing or the most powerful self-acceptance.

The shoulders also hold a variety of energy points, but when we do healing onto the shoulder, we work on connecting to the soft tissue of the shoulders. This also creates a release around the neck and throat which is enhanced by the heat released from the healer's hands. Once again,

I do believe this works and is a great healing technique, but it will also need many sessions to be of long term benefit.

## PART 3

I have, since this first time, seen into people's bodies on many occasions. I have precisely pointed out cracked bones in hands and shoulders. I have tested myself and scanned people's bodies and, more often than not, am right with what I find. I have been able to tell if people have had other psychic surgeons or spiritual healings before and can sometimes even tell who the healer was who has done the healing.

*I am aware this is not really me seeing into the body. I am just seeing second hand information from the spirit doctors or surgeons that are working with me.*

*I see trauma in the body as coloured jelly beans. The jelly bean shape is not as important to me but the colour is relevant to me. If the trauma bean is red, it is an active trauma, as it fades in colour it becomes less active, and if it is clear it is a dormant trauma but is still in the body and probably affecting the client. What I mean by a dormant trauma is that the client has moved on from the trauma, has dealt with the issue mentally but it has not been released from the body.*

*These clear types of trauma are often found with older clients who have accepted themselves, or clients who are proactively working on themselves - either on their own or with other therapists. I believe the process of healing oneself must not only be a mental process it must be continued from thought down into the body. I call this 'downloading' and I do get a large proportion of clients who just need me to help them download the already known information from their brain to their body. Interestingly enough, healers are commonly the people I work on who just need me to help them download. Downloading can have a very powerful, quick response in a client and I am often warranted with the stature of being the person who created the healing. I am very quick to stop this belief that it's me doing the work.*

*As I have said before and will probably say over and over again - I am just the helper. I am not the healer. The healing happens because the client chooses to come and see me. All I am doing is the job that I have agreed to do with my guides. I am not responsible for anyone's healing other than my own.*

*I believe that many psychological therapies neglect the body and only try and work on the brain. I also think they neglect the fact that most of the trauma is in the child part of the person's psyche and they work with the adult or the parent part of the person's psyche. I work with every client seeking out where in their energy I will find the childhood trauma.*

*Almost all traumas can be traced back to the first 7 years of life. Now please be aware that I am generalising and that there are many incredibly good therapists that do understand all of this too.*

## PART 4

What I found around Rachel's eyes is very common. We create our own lives through our beliefs; Rachel had become so afraid that she created a belief in her that she may not see the future. She 'may not see' are the words that became energetically connected to her eyes. She was slowly but surely creating a blinding energetic in front of her eyes. I believe that if it had been on her body for much longer, it would have reached the inner eye and would have then become far more serious.

*When I moved to Rachel's ears, it became apparent that the energy in her ears was that of the type that would not move; her hearing would continue to deteriorate unless she dealt with a huge amount of childhood issues that probably started before she was born, and then reiterated over and over again in her life until she was 100% certain that she did not deserve to be heard.*

*An interesting point to make here is that I have noticed*

*that if a client comes to see me with large hoop earrings, or very long dangly earrings, I will also know that they had not been heard by their parents.*

*When I first discovered this I would actually stop strangers in the street who were wearing large earrings and politely enquire if they felt their parents listened to their needs, and with clients and strangers, I have 100% accuracy with this belief. I have learned that we never choose jewellery because we love the way it looks, but rather the way it feels on our body.*

*We use jewellery to fine tune the energetics of our body without realising we are doing it. This is why I prefer my clients to be free of metal on their body. This way, when I am doing the healing session, I can see through any of their own self-tunings that they do not even know they are using.*

*On several occasions I have had clients who have taken off jewellery before a session and then never worn that jewellery again after the session.*

## PART 5

Over the years that I have been seeing clients, I have learnt that some of the work I am doing is so powerful on the body's energy that over-doing it can leave a client more unstable. This is not a good thing. It may end up being more beneficial for a client, but what I have found is that a client should feel that change has happened during the session and that more change is going to happen in the next few days. I do not want a client to leave feeling totally wiped out. Sometimes this is inevitable, but then I will sit with the client and ground them through me for the last few minutes of the session. However, as clients become more used to the way I work, and they have less powerful traumas to shift, or they are good at shifting them, then I start to offer even longer sessions.

I find an hour is enough for the first session with a client, but after a long-term treatment, over months and years, those clients have more information for me to hear, more understanding, and we need more time to get into the more in-depth energetic blocks that may be affecting them.

## PART 6

Through the thousands of readings I have given as a Medium, and the thousands of clients I have seen for spiritual healing, as well as my own interest in the universe and humanities role on earth, I have come up with my own beliefs about life on earth.

I believe that earth is a space created by intention of the universe, the universe's ultimate goal is to grow and learn more about itself, to understand itself better. I believe spirit in the universe, or parts of the universe that have individual identity, experience existence at an extremely high vibration.

This means that when the universe experiences happiness, sadness, jealousy, envy, lust, enlightenment, it's so fleeting that it's hard for the universe to get a full grasp of the feeling; the sensations are so quick they are not really fulfilling. The universe craves sensation, so through its intention, a space has been created where parts of the universe (souls) get the chance of being connected to a heavy slow energetic vibration (physical body) to be involved in these fleeting emotions in a much more intense, longer lasting experience.

As humans, we feel everything so intensely because our space or plane is so dense and slow, so the vibrations of our emotions affect us far more deeply and allow our souls to experience the true nature of emotions and feelings. This is why I always tell people that all our emotions are important.

With Rachel I explained this to her, I made her aware that she, as a soul, had chosen this path and thus, although she may be dying, she is, in my opinion, just going home where she will be back in her high vibrational, normal atmosphere and will be able to still be a part of her family's lives.

I explained to Rachel that dying can be painful and scary but that death itself is instant and that it's a soft, warm and freeing experience for her body to go through. Everything on earth comes here to die. Death is the only normal thing on earth next to life, but most humans have just not yet grasped that normality of it. I felt that this helped Rachel to not be so afraid and she had instead thought through her fear of death rather than dwelling on it. I made sure that Rachel knew that this was my point of view on life and death and that she must choose for herself what to believe.

## PART 7

On millennium eve I went with a good friend, Tee, to see her friends and wish them happy New Year. Tee's friends lived with their grandmother whom I had met a few times before. On that night, as her grandmother walked into the room we were in, I saw the image of a skeleton over her body that was so extremely powerful I could hardly see the lady herself. After leaving I said to Tee that I had seen death with her friend's grandmother and that I expected it to come to her soon. That night, just after the New Year had come in, Tee's friend's grandmother passed away. "I have seen death", is what I said to Rachel, "but I do not see death with you right now. I have seen death before and been right."

## PART 8

*When it comes to how many sessions I should see a client for, sometimes it's as simple as my guides telling me this client needs 4 sessions but then I will tell them four sessions at first with the caveat that more may be needed if we unearth more stuff to work on during the sessions.*

*Mostly I want to see a client for 2 initial sessions before deciding if the client needs more sessions. First sessions get the client comfortable with the dynamic of working with me, finding my place of work, basically getting over the first fears and the unknowns of seeing me. Amazingly, even clients who are used to seeing healers and therapists get really nervous coming to see me. I don't bite, actually I am very physically gentle; energetically I can be extremely brutal if needed.*

*In a first session I usually can get into the actual issue but the second session is where I believe the deep work begins to happen. In most cases, by the time the client has come for their second session, they already know that I can help them and that the healing has worked. They may not be able to understand it totally but they know things have changed.*

*So in the second session they are far more open than the*

first session, consequently, the work gets deeper. I find second sessions can often just be energy transfer because the client is open to healing themselves with my help.

Often the client knows they need more sessions or they choose one more session just as a backup. I usually would suggest that clients come and see me when, and if, they need me. What I find happens with this is they end up coming to me when they are so deep in their issue they need rescuing, so I now suggest frequent maintenance sessions to stop clients from getting so deep into their issues.  This also holds a thread of connection with the client, so they feel that there is help out there if they need it.

I suggest a 6 week period of maintenance on a continuous basis, or until the client knows without a doubt that they no longer need to see me. I take no offense to this; it means they have moved on and grown and hopefully, with my help, learned the tools they need to deal with their life's ups and downs.

It is always good feedback when a client calls after not having seen me for a few years and says that since their last session was so good, they could now recognise that they needed help and knew they needed to call me.

With Rachel it becomes important to focus on the extreme maintenance of her emotional stability; her emotional state can be far more detrimental to her than the actual state of *her body. Her mind has the power over her body at this point. If Rachel feels supported, having support from her family and friends will help her, but she also needs someone who she can vent her emotions to without that person getting emotionally hurt or involved, someone who can handle their emotions while Rachel expresses hers. That someone is often me with my clients, but most definitely with Rachel.*

*I have had a 90 year old client lay into me with all he was worth in connection to his illness; he needed a person to vent at, and he needed to get it out. I sat and listened to him, I allowed myself to be open to his release and accepted him and understood he needed to release. I held a space for his need. As the session came to an end he turned to me and, with tears in his eyes, apologised for venting at me and then said: "you are the only one I can really tell my fears to."*

*Because of this, I accepted Rachel's idea of seeing me every two weeks until she felt she did not need me any longer, or she could work towards 6 weeks maintenance.*

## CONCLUSION

Rachel was a person who was very passionate about her life and family. I could easily see why she had become ill; she held almost all her childhood trauma within her and owned it all. I also believe she felt responsible for her children's trauma too. I think our first session together had gone well and I believed we would have some changes for her. She felt better to me and she told me she felt different, so it was a good place to start moving forward from. I could also sense a new energy from Rachel - energy of cheekiness or naughtiness. This would be something I would look forward to seeing when she came to see me again.

*I try to not get emotionally involved with all my clients, but I am human, so it's important for me that after a session with a client is over, I release the energetics. If I remember parts of a session the next day it's because there is still more work to be done, either related to me or to the client. Sometimes the lines become thinner that separate me from my clients.*

*This happens when a client has been to see me many times and I have established a genuine openness between me and the client which has become closer to a friendship. With this I will allow a friendship to organically start if it is meant to be.*

*The way I work with clients is that I am open and honest with all my own issues. I want my clients to see that I am a real person who hurts and burps and messes up just like everyone else.*

*I use my personal experiences to explain energetics and*

*healing to my clients and I am not afraid to talk about anything: I talk to clients about energy, illness, love, life, sex and even have many times taught an alternative understanding of the importance of proper masturbation. I have a client who has seen me for over 60 sessions (her choice), who I now regard as my friend. I have clients who are now work colleagues and I have one client who ended up becoming my partner, mother of my son, ex-partner and the most important friend I have ever had.*

*I hold my boundaries with most clients like rods of steel, but I have to allow those rods to soften at times; it's the right thing to do. Once again, I can only be responsible for my own energetics; I cannot be responsible for other people's choices in life.*

## SESSION 2

A brief breakdown of Rachel's second session:

Two weeks after her first session, Rachel arrived full of smiles. She told me that since her last session she had been feeling very upbeat and her fears had decreased considerably.

Rachel told me that by the evening after her first session, her eyesight had returned back to normal and that she spent the next few days reading everything she could just in case her eyesight went away again.

Slowly, I was starting to see the comical and cheeky side of Rachel, and our session became quite humorous. I do not know if I can write the humour down and give it justice. It may have been one of those situations where you had to be there.

I spent time with Rachel talking about her feelings since her last session and working on her energetics, clearing the last of the shock from her body. Her change from being so despondent to more upbeat had proven to be a great help in increasing the release of shock. Rachel did not look like a person waiting for death anymore.

With a very serious and scared face, Rachel asked me, near the end of her session, if I thought she was dying. I told Rachel that yes, just like the rest of us, you are dying, but not just yet, I said I believe there is more time for her. This is a question that Rachel would come to ask me every session and every session I would answer in the same way. "Rachel just like the rest of us, you are dying, but not just yet."

Rachel left full of beans and living life again, she had begun painting and moving about again. She had also found a new home to live in and was busy getting ready to move. I can see that the first session had given Rachel the help she needed to start living again. It is almost as if the session had given her permission to live again.

*There is no possible way I could ever know what the outcome of a session may be. I have had clients who have not noticed any changes for weeks after their session and then one day realise they are different. I have had clients throwing up after a session, or sleeping for hours and hours after a session. We are all so different that I refrain from guessing what will happen after a session. Most clients know immediately that there has been change, some realise that, all of a sudden, they are being emotional and that they are releasing more emotions than normal, some clients have pain vanish within a few days of the session.*

*Some clients come back with far worse symptoms because all the protection around their trauma has been cleared out and it's open for a more in-depth healing. I usually just tell my clients to expect that they may be overly emotional over the next week and to accept those emotions and changes and allow them to release.*

*A lady client, who is larger than life and often in the public eye, had come and seen me for a session. At the end of the session I said that I thought that she should expect to be emotional over the next few days. The following afternoon she called me:*

*"Wayne darling" she said, "you were wrong. I am not emotional today. I have never felt happier in my life."*

*I simply said: "But happiness **is** an emotion."*

*She said laughing "oh yeah!!"*

*It was good to see the positive changes that had come with Rachel's first session. I am thankful for my guides and my ability; it is nice to help in the way I am able to help.*

## Session 3

**Quiet session with loads of healing and grounding.**

## Session 4

(8 weeks after I first met Rachel)

Rachel arrived in her normal manner of humour and awkward hugs. She looked healthy and active and had lost a little weight because she had been so much more active. Rachel told me that she had been to the hospital to have her final scan after the operation making sure that everything they had done was working properly. During the scan they found that a piece of tubing had broken off one of the medical tools they had used during the operation and was curled up in a spiral in her stomach.

The doctors were very surprised and shocked as they say that had never happened before and that it was not supposed to be able to happen with that particular piece of equipment.

Rachel was not surprised, she immediately realised that the pipe was the spiral I had seen in her stomach during her first session. The next day the doctors put a thin surgical cable with a clamp on the end down through her nose into her stomach and in a 5 minute procedure they very easily removed the tube that was curled up in her stomach

*This was a very good confirmation for me of the belief I have in myself and in my guides. As I write this I feel like I must remember to continue to always trust my intuition. It has never led me astray.*

Rachel became a friend, but was always a client. She needed me to be her healer more than she needed me to be her friend and we both knew it. I am going to tell you about a few humorous sessions we had together.

I was helping Rachel with her courage, to stand up to her husband who she had been separated from for many years. She wanted a divorce so she could get the money she deserved out of the house she jointly owned with him. Rachel believed that her husband was literally waiting for her to die so he could get the other half of the house for himself.

I was working with Rachel on her fears of standing up to her husband through the divorce. Helping her clear her fears of her father and mother to allow her to stand up for herself. Now please remember that Rachel's hearing was not always very good.

She arrived for her session and early on in the session I asked her:

"Rachel how is the divorce going?"

Rachel said: "It died."

I asked, confused, how a divorce could die: "Why did the divorce die?"

She calmly said: "because I fed it an apple."

By this time I was totally confused; I asked her what she was talking about. She told me that when she was young, she had a horse and had fed the horse an apple and for some reason she did not understand, the apple had caused the horse's death.

I said: "What horse?" "I asked about your divorce." "Ohhhh" replied Rachel!

Rachel had another fight on her hands that she was dealing with throughout the years of our sessions: a fight with smoking. I am glad to say that she did beat it in the end, but there were many hours that she spent with me, asking me if it's ok for her to smoke, to not tell her children she was smoking again. She would come to see me about stopping smoking for her children, and then spend the session telling me why she liked smoking so much. I never told her to stop smoking, I just listened. Truly, I was amazed when one day, she just stopped.

Rachel arrived one day feeling a little light headed, like she was spinning. I asked why she thought she was feeling this way. She said because she had decided that it was wrong for her to still be taking anti-depressants and that after over 10 years of taking them, she decided to stop, so she just threw them away and stopped. I asked her if she realised that she should have weaned herself off them slowly. She said she could not be bothered with that and just stopped.

It took a good few weeks for her to stop spinning and feeling like she was floating, as her body got used to the extreme change from taking the drugs.

Rachel told me that if she was 20 years younger that I would be her next husband.

Rachel asked me about her eye infections. Intuitively, I got that she must use only new makeup products on her eyes and must throw away her old stuff because they may be holding the bacteria that is affecting her eyes. Rachel told me that she loved her eyeliners and could not possibly throw them away; she had had some of them for over 35 years.

Over two years into seeing Rachel on and off once or twice a month, Rachel dropped the bomb on me that the cancer nurse had said that only 10% of people with her kind of cancer and who had had the type of operation that she had, had survived more than two years after the operation.

She asked me if she was going to die soon. I asked her how she was feeling; she said the best she had felt since her operation. I said, if you are feeling good and are doing good, then I see no reason for you not to keep on living longer; obviously you are in that 10% that do live longer.

Rachel said "that's good, but could you please not tell my children cause I like the way they treat me when they think I am dying."

Rachel developed a back pain that caused her to seek medical advice again. She was diagnosed with cancer again. It was about three years of me being privileged enough to know Rachel and her family. Over the following months Rachel turned to medication to help control the pain. She was a fighter.

Sophia emailed me and asked if I would go and see Rachel at her home again. Only this time, she asked if I could help Rachel move on. Rachel's pain was too much and Rachel had decided she wanted to finish her fight.

On a Friday I went to see her and her family. I sat with her, open just like I did the day we met. I accepted her and I held the energy for her to allow her to change. Rachel had decided it was enough pain, enough fighting and had come to terms with life and death. I also did sessions with her son and daughter that day. Holding energy for them so they could allow change to happen too.

On the following Monday, I received a text message from Rachel's daughter, that Rachel had passed away peacefully.

I was so privileged to meet such a wonderful loving, caring, interesting woman and her family. I was asked to be at the funeral and to say some words about Rachel. I had come to know her better than maybe even her closest friends knew her.

I knew Rachel would be there watching over her funeral and she showed us by making her picture fall during the ceremony. I will never forget the powerful women that she was. I so appreciate the lessons she taught me.

Thank you Rachel

## TESTIMONIAL

This is a testimonial from Rachel's sister after she read this case study.

### My thoughts of Rachel's sessions with Wayne from her sister, Amanda

To understand the level of help that Wayne provided for Rachel is hard to describe without first mentioning a bit about Rachel. Rachel looked fragile and almost gave an air of helplessness, and this made us protect her even more. She had a hard life and was not treated kindly by the men in her life - and in the last ten years of her life, she devoted herself to her family and her grandchildren. We loved her fiercely. She was the kindest person you could ever meet. She was eccentric and had a wicked sense of humour. When she was diagnosed with pancreatic cancer aged just 59, she did not want to know the seriousness of the disease, or that only 3 per cent of people live past 5 years. Her operation to remove the cancer took 12 hours and she didn't want to know about the operation or how many organs they were removing. She went into the theatre like she was having her appendix out.

That is when things went wrong. She woke up in intensive care in Southampton with frightening hallucinations and they carried on for three days. She was terrified and her son had to stay by her bedside at night to stop her from pulling out all the tubes. When she got home she was terrified of dying and terrified of the drugs she would be given at the end of her life. She was not recovering and that was when her friend Linda called Wayne. The difference in her was amazing. When Wayne said that there was something wrong in her tummy area and the surgeons rescanned her

– they called her in to say that they had left a piece of tubing in her tummy we just could not believe it.

Wayne continued to see her for the four years we had left with Rachel. Each time he saw her, she became brighter and had more energy. He helped her come to terms with her past and most importantly, a few days before she died, he helped her to come to peace with dying and let go. She did not want to leave her family, was terrified of dying and just would not let go. He took tremendous pressure off us as a family just by his presence. I can categorically say that without Wayne we would not have had the quality of life we had with Rachel in the last four years. She needed Wayne spiritually and emotionally, and thank god he was there.

Amanda.

# ALEX AND THE FOETAL BULLING

## OVERVIEW

In this case study we begin to explore how, as humans, we establish our strongest human beliefs and patterns from conception through into our childhood. These beliefs affect who we are and control us in our adult life. We explore the amazing realisation that beliefs that where created whilst in the womb also affect our futures. We touch on how, just by realising that we are not at fault for our childhood traumas, we can easily change our future.

Alex is from a loving, caring family but, unlike his siblings, life seems to be punishing him. He comes across with energy of having been severely bullied. He shows that he has been fighting his own private internal war, wondering why he is different to his family.

Through intuition, understanding and releases of trauma from before his birth, a huge turnaround is created that changes his life and gives him the confidence to move forward without fear.

## BOOKING

Alex's session was booked by his mother over the phone.

*Because the session is booked by Alex's mother I must check with him if he is here of his own free will. I can't help anyone if they are there for someone else.*

*Often a female client will come and see me and a week later her husband will be walking up my driveway, usually a little slower and less enthusiastically than I would want. With these clients I always ask the first question; "Do you want to be here; are you here of your own free will?" I have only once had a husband say no and I then offered for him to go home and tell his wife I could not work with him because it needs to be his total choice and not one pushed on him. The same applies to children over 13-15 years of age, depending on their maturity.*

*I once had a client arrive in a total state of shock; he was around 15 and was sent by his mum to see his friends for a weekend in London, from his home in Europe. The family friend who he was staying with in London picked him up from the airport and brought him directly to see me. Only when they arrived at me was he told that he had an appoint-*

*ment and was ushered inside. He was not amused and to-*
*tally confused. I offered for him to go and not have the ses-*
*sion. I told him that I would deal with his mother if there*
*were any repercussions with his choice. He decided to try it*
*out and, at the end of the session, asked if it would be pos-*
*sible to come and see me again, and I agreed.*

## MY PREPARATION

I am intuitively aware that I must watch Alex's arrival
for his session. I am strongly aware that I need to be gentle,
this is extremely important with Alex. I can feel that any
closed judgement towards him, would close him down. I
can feel his energetics a good 15 minutes before the session. I can sense his uncertainty, deep anxiety and his
hopefulness.

*I always keep awareness over myself knowing that even*
*48 hours before a session I can be picking up information*
*about, or for, a client. If something does come through, I al-*
*ways make note of it, mentally, but do not hold onto it, as it*
*may be a projection of fear or anxiety from the client that is*
*not relevant for me to bring into their session. If it is relevant*
*it will make itself clear during the session and then I will*
*know that it is essential to work on with my client.*

*I have discovered that many of my clients will have a distinct reaction in the 24 hours prior to coming to see me. I remember a client once cancelled her session 4 weeks in a row because, the morning before, she felt odd and thought it best not to see me. On the fourth week I pointed out to her that maybe the pattern is that the healing is starting a day early for her and she must see me no matter how she is feeling. She took this on-board and came to see me despite how she felt. Her session was one I will never forget, the energy movements were phenomenal, and even affected the physical room with inexplicable flashing lights and sounds! The outcomes for her were also powerful, she, who was separating from her long-term partner, transformed herself then within two month, then got back together with that same partner, in a new, much more productive relationship - which is still progressing today, many years later.*

*Just because the healing session is scheduled at a certain time, it does not mean that there is no energetic preparation before the session, or continued healing after the session. Just making the booking is in itself a step into healing. It's a message to the client's soul and body, from the client's consciousness, that it is in need of, and open to, healing and thus healing begins. They are accepting their own personal need for help and accepting themselves as they are.*

*Since my guides and spirit doctors lead me, there is always the possibility of healing happening in weird and strange ways. I have even had a client cancel her session because, just a few hours after she made the booking, her long-standing problem of extreme headaches started to ease, and eventually, within a day, were gone. Her self-realisation that she needed help, for her headaches, and her actively seeking help by making the appointment with me, a healer, created the space and intention of healing, and thus she took the steps forward that healed her headaches.*

*It is important for us to be aware that whatever happens, happens for a reason, and is relevant. If a client comes late, it's relevant, if a client cancels it's relevant, if a bumble bee flies into the window while I am working, it's relevant. I have been with a client in my healing room at home and noticed a black car randomly stop outside my house; the lady in the car removed her seat belt, took off her jumper, replaced her seat belt then motioned a religious cross across her chest and drove off. To me, this event could not have been random, it may have been random for the lady in the car, but for me it was extremely important. It was also important for my client, because my client was also watching the event as it unfolded. I turned to my client and said that the car was relevant for her and that she must allow the changes of healing to happen (allow change - black car. Black is the end of old and the beginning of new), she must not be afraid to step forward into new ground (removing the seat belt), allow yourself to be vulnerable (removing jumper), she would be safe no matter how vulnerable she felt (replacing seat belt), and then she must believe in herself (crossing the chest). All these things made total sense to both of us, with relevance to the client's personal situation. I explained to my client that her guides had actively created that to happen for her. The fact that she was seeking help, was the right move for her. That was affirmation that she was in the right place, going in the right direction. If she was not, she would never have been here watching all this unfold. Knowing you are where you are supposed to be in your life is in itself a huge healing realisation and release.*

*Everything that happens in a session, everything, is relevant. Just imagine how much effort the universe had gone to for my client. It arranged for the lady to need to take off her jumper at that exact time and to do it outside my house. It seems like a tall order, but when these occurrences happen so often, you begin to wonder whether anything is ever by chance?*

*I have had the weirdest of events happen during a session; from foxes standing on walls, 3 massive black birds in the tree outside, strange sounds, sirens going off outside (when in the 5 years before that I had never heard a siren go off ), flashing lights, insects arriving, smells, clicking noises, swaying window blinds, and many more. I believe these happen because I allow myself to be aware of them and allow my intuition to accept them; it makes no difference if these strange happenings are right or not, but it has always helped me.*

*During a session if I am drawn to a client's jewellery or the colour of clothing the client has worn, if a phrase keeps going through my head, or I get nursery rhymes or songs (this happens sometimes), I pay attention - these things are relevant.*

*So, in conclusion, I am always aware of what is happening in, and around, the session I am busy with. Everything is relevant and, as the healer, I need to be open to all messages, no matter how they are delivered.*

## ARRIVAL

I noticed a deep sadness within my client as he approached the house and, as he greeted me, I could feel his anxiety and his fear of being discovered, a fear I could see through him. His mum arrived with him and asked if she could sit in the session. This is unusual for a 24 year old male to have his mum in a session with him but, from past experience, I know to allow what the client wants. I allow the client to take the lead as this will help me to help him. I ask him if he wants his mum in the session, and he readily agrees. It felt right to me too, as they seemed to have a very close bond and connection.

I was aware that he was unable to keep total eye contact with me and I was also aware that the energetics around his base chakra were heavier than they should be. I could feel the huge energy pushing down on his shoulders, the points of self-expectation, like he was trying to hold up the world.

*Every time a client arrives, I like to greet them at the front door and walk behind them as they walk to the session room. This way I get to see them walk, feel the trail of their energy and get an energetic connection before we even start the session. I have often pin-pointed a client's issue, almost immediately, during the walk to the healing room. I recall a client who was 3 years old when he came to see me; his mum was worried about his unusual mood swings and behaviour. I noticed immediately that he was lagging his left leg behind him, as he walked. Following inspection of his legs, I noted a difference in his leg length and the feel of the energy in his base chakra. I assumed he had a hip problem that was either creating strain on his body and making him tired, or actually causing pain, or both. I realised that this would also need a physical intervention and, as I am not qualified to do this, we organised a McTimoney chiropractor for him. After a few treatments he was walking better and his behaviour had stabilised because he was no longer over tired or in pain. What was even more interesting though, was when his mother came to see me for a session, I found the same problem with her hip and she also found relief from a variety of her ailments through the same chiropractor. I often find parents and children mimic or mirror each other's ailments, and healing one, can very possibly heal the other.*

*I would like to note that the chances are quite strong that the young boy had experienced his hip problem from birth. Since he was never aware that he was in pain, and there-fore unable to share this fact with his mum, one can assume that he had become used to the pain and that it was the norm due to its longevity.*

## BASIC INFORMATION

Male, 24 years of age. Slight of body, but muscular (wiry). No specific early life religion. Older sister and younger sister. All approximately 3 years apart. Both sisters doing well.

*The basic info I take is always the same and I always*

*try to write as little down as possible. I do not take notes during or after a session, all these case studies come from being imprinted in my mind. I believe writing too much down creates an energetic imprint and can hold the client in the same energy. What I do write down, I often just put through my shredder anyway. The things I always ask are:*

- *Client's name at birth;*
- *Client's current age;*
- *The current age and gender of their siblings;*
- *The religion they grew up following.*
- *How they heard about me?*
- *What their reasons are for seeing me?*

### Client's birth name:

*The client's birth name is important. I have had a client who, after three sessions, was not getting anywhere and, for me, three sessions without any kind of breakthrough, is very rare. Three months later she was drawn to come back to me for another session. From the beginning of that session my guides kept asking me to ask her what her name is. I found this peculiar as I knew her name already, but my guides were very persistent so I obliged and asked her why my guides would keep asking me to ask her name. She told me she had changed her name as soon as she had turned eighteen because she wanted to disconnect from the memories of her awful upbringing. With her permission, I did the rest of the session using her birth name and we had a very productive trauma releasing session. The reason for this is that at eighteen she had actively separated her trauma from her body by changing her name. She has been in a constant disconnection from her childhood trauma and for the first three sessions we were just working on the mask and not on the true trauma and issues. When I focused on her real name I triggered her real trauma hence creating reactions.*

*During a session I will often ask clients different questions relating to their name, or for married women, their maiden names but only if I am drawn to it, or it's put into my mind, by my guides and spirit doctors.*

### Sibling's age and gender:

*It is always important to know what was happening for my clients when they where children. Sibling rivalry can be an important bit of information that I have in my store of knowledge connected with the client. This kind of knowledge can give me hints into understanding the client's patterns. It's about putting myself in their shoes from conception to the present; an understanding of the persons entire make up. I like to get a feeling of their energy from as many aspects as possible; physical ailments, energetic traumas, personal beliefs and childhood beliefs. What I conceive about the family dynamic is so very vast, but also very specific to each client; one person's childhood trauma can be another person's most important childhood lesson.*

*Most of the dynamics that create who we are, are based on our childhood energetics that are created when we were under seven years of age, starting from pre-conception; the intention parents have for getting pregnant. The years before our seventh birthday are all part of our unconscious development. Unconscious development is when the child is learning all the basics of being a human being. Physically; how to breathe, cry, feed, swallow, blink, sit, stand, walk, communicate, cuddle etc. Behaviourally; the child is learning how to behave in all the situations that it has witnessed its parents in. Emotionally they are learning if emotions are allowed, which emotions are nice and which are not so nice, which are accepted and which are rejected, they are taking on everything emotionally from their parents, family and peers.*

*I believe that the child, from conception to 7 years of age, has a greater capacity to understand energy and that they communicate energetically, learning from all the energetic messages that adults no longer realise they are processing. The child is trying to learn to survive in its family and our society.*

*When a child is young they learn things like: how mums treat dads, how dads treat mums, how sisters treat brothers, how friends treat friends, how to show love to a partner/ sister/ brother, how to be intimate, how to react to trauma, how to accept love, how to behave in millions of different situations; basically they are creating their subconscious selves. The child begins to learn their patterns of beliefs and behaviour that will be their adulthood and how they, as individuals, connect to each other in family, love, work and friendship. All these have been taught to the child from conception. It is a proven fact that a child is born with an accent in their cry, it's completely obvious we start learning to be human at conception.*

### Religion followed while growing up.

*As well as positive habits, I find that certain religions that are taught to people in their childhood can leave negative habits that can affect the client deep into their adulthood. The most common belief that I find associated with religion that causes trauma in a client is, "I am a sinner". With this knowledge I can help release this trauma for the client.*

### How did you hear about me?

I usually ask this for new clients like Alex, however, I already knew that Alex's mum had brought her parents and suggested to some of her friends to see me.

*How a client finds out about me is very important for me, as well as, why and how they choose to see me. Knowing how a client finds me can often tell me that other clients are happy with the sessions they have had; when you see a new client and in the next few days every one of their family and friends is calling you, you can be quite sure the session was good for them and they have already had a positive outcome. This is not important to me on an ego basis, it's more important to me that what I am doing is working, because I take every session to be as important as the next, and I do my very best for my client without really worrying what the client thinks or feels about the sessions.*

*I am not responsible for my clients healing, I am only responsible for giving my client the best I can do in the time I see them, when they leave it's all up to them again. It is important for me to abide by this, because if I do not, then I am allowing myself to keep giving to the client energetically and that is not fair on them or me.*

*The only way I wish to work, is for clients to be intuitively, instinctively drawn to me, to have an overpowering gut feeling I can help them. However, this is not always the case, not all my clients are able to distinguish between their feelings and thoughts and, often, fear or boundaries placed by society, religion and family get in the way. Often I meet someone and I know they need to see me, I feel it in my gut, but, it's not up to me to tell them. I have to let them go and hope they find me of their own free will, if that is right for them. I never chase a client, even if I know I can help them.*

*We are responsible for our own healing we need to be the ones who choose who we ask to help us through healing. As a healer I let people choose me and then I do not take re-sponsibility for their choice. Let me clarify this part again. A client who chooses to see me is 100% responsible for their own healing. As the healer, all I can do is my very best throughout the time period of the healing. I never call or speak to my clients outside session hours, other than with the odd client I know needs to have a text or call to check in on them, for example, if they are going through a divorce or illness and are feeling totally alone (maybe 1% of my clients get this from me and it will be my guides who tell me who is in need of it). I am, as a healer, not responsible for the out-come of the healing session.*

*Let me explain with an example: My rule for helping cli-ents who wish to stop smoking is simple, before you come and see me, you must not have smoked at all for over 3 days and must be craving cigarettes. After the session, you must not smoke for at least 24 hours. If the client goes to their car after their intense 1 hour stop-smoking session with me, and immediately lights up and smokes again as they pull away, or any time there after, effectively undoing all the work we have done together in the session, then how could it possibly be my, the healer's, responsibility?*

*We are all responsible for our own healing process. I feel a level of sadness for our poor doctors out there who have taken an oath to be responsible for all those patients who are not willing to take responsibility for themselves (I sometimes fall into this category too, but try my best not to depend on my doctors without knowing what is happening to my own body). We give our doctors all our personal power and put our lives in their very "human" hands. Yes, doctors do have more medical knowledge than us, but they are not us. How can we blame them for our health not improving, or for our lack of healing? It is always up to us if we heal or not, we need to take responsibility for our own lives and wellbeing.*

*My client session starts and ends and there is nothing after. If there is information in connection with that client coming to me after their session, then I know the client is either talking about me, or there is something in me that I need to work on in connection to what that client is going through. This may surprise many of you reading this, but my deepest belief is that: **All healing is self-healing**.*

*As I work with my clients and help them heal, I will focus on individual issues or traumas in that client. If, however, I have a similar issue in me and I feel the energetics also awaken in me, I can choose to allow the healing to be for both of us, or at least begin the healing within myself. During a session I always focus on the clients needs but I also know that if I have a similar block to the client, and I release it, the action of releasing my personal blocks will help in the release of the clients block too. On many occasions, whilst working with a client I will actually reach into my own energy field and facilitate a release from a chakra, or I'll write down beliefs for me to work on later after the client's session. As I have mentioned previously, all healing is self-healing and I appreciate that clients bring me their issues so that I may also become aware of my own issues. Without this awareness and help from my clients, I doubt I would be so self-aware.*

### *Reasons for a client coming to see me:*

Alex tells me that he is uncertain of himself. He has this deep overpowering feeling that everything he does is wrong and he is unable to cope in our society because of it. He struggles to hold his motivation. He is uncertain in his sexual orientation. He does not feel like he is supposed to be alive and has attempted to take his own life and has a history of drug use. Self-confidence is non-existent and he finds himself becoming dependent on his girlfriends and family for recognition. Alex said he felt numb, he could not feel his feelings and it felt like he walked through his life in as a kind of zombie.

*I always ask a client why they have chosen to see me, I actually almost always use those exact words for a new client; "Why have you chosen to come and see me?" The reason I use those words is because it creates an opening of the energetic connection with the client. When they answer that precise question they are accepting my terms and conditions. When they answer the question they have acknowledged that it's their choice to be in the session and so have opened themselves to healing. They have, energetically, given me permission to help them for the highest of good beyond my understanding. This allows the energy to begin to truly move.*

*On the other hand, I also never take what my client is saying as total truth. If I 'listen' to them and accept what the client is telling me, I may have created a smoke screen that I may never be able to get past. Clients often sabotage their own healing without even knowing they are doing it. Because of this, I work on 'hearing' the client. I must hear them not only with my ears, but also with my entire body. It is through the energy that I can truly hear them. The things they say that hit me energetically, throughout my body, are important. Any thought, feeling, memory, physical reaction and outside reaction that happens is relevant to the client.*

*I have had clients tell me how wonderful their parents were; that they could not ask for better parents, and then 20 minutes later, they are full of tears as I have them repeating their inner beliefs over and over again; "I am responsible for my parents happiness".*

*Often clients do not want to face the truth about their own childhoods. For a person to realise that they have changed the way they behave to keep their parents happy all their lives, is a very big self-discovery, just the acknowledgment of this is a huge energetic release for a client. Therefore, I can never take what a client says as total truth. I cannot trust what they intellectually think as opposed to what their actual inner child beliefs are. The person I trust during a session is myself. If I hear the body say something to me, then it's true. Through the thousands of clients I have seen and whose bodies I have listened to, I am confident in this. Often, a client will deny the actual internal childhood belief that I hear, but the beliefs I am working on are not about the adult client that is laying on the healing couch in front of me, they are beliefs usually created when that client was in their unconscious awareness stage under seven years of age.*

*These are the beliefs I find that make a difference when you work on them, the younger the better - some beliefs even come from before birth.*

## INITIAL ASSESSMENT

My instant feeling from Alex is that I would like him as a person. I feel he is far more intelligent that he realises. I see a good upbringing and caring parents and grandparents. I can see that he is totally confused why his life has turned out this way and why he cannot seem to keep it together. I feel that he is genuine. I know Alex has tried his best and feels guilty about his life.

*I have learned how to use my feelings through a session, how to check-in with myself as we go through the session and use these feelings to understand where my client is at any point. With Alex, I knew I could be his friend, I knew he was a genuine guy just trying to do his best. I learnt to use this through a client who was a model. She was very beautiful to look at, but when she came for a session, I was actually afraid to touch her energetically and physically, she actually repulsed me. I took this as a sign of her not feeling really nice inside and being full of trauma, sadness, and hurt. We did three sessions together and by the time we got to the third session, I was again afraid to touch her, but this time I was worried I might find her desirable. Her past trauma had been released and she now showed her inner beauty and femininity.*

*Trusting my feelings in connection with a client's trauma allows me to delve quickly and deeply into their energetics, hoping to help them for the highest of good.*

**Energetic messages from the initial assessment.**

These are the messages I picked up from Alex's body, messages that came to me whilst I was connected to him.

- I am not good enough
- It's all me
- It's all my fault
- I need to be told I am ok
- Everyone is better than me
- I never get heard
- I can't cope

These Basic beliefs are ones that I regularly hear from a person's body when they have low self-esteem, but I am aware that I am missing something. Alex was not brought up by parents who would instil this in him, and both his parents are positive school teachers. He gives off the same feeling as I would expect from someone who has been severely bullied, but through questioning him, he does not remember actually being bullied in any extreme way at all. I was expecting bullying by a family member or by unspoken family expectation, but there was none of that, and his other siblings are doing well. I also considered that he was the only son, but he had a good relationship with his dad and granddad. I was very drawn to connect with his very heavy base chakra; I knew it was going to be the key to his issue. It was so profoundly different to the other energy in his body that it must be where he holds his trauma and the secret to helping him heal. It was time to get to it and get on the couch.

*I find it hard to tell if my brain or body receives the beliefs, or even if it's intuitive and/or received through my guides, but I know that the more I work, the more I am able to understand the dynamics of human patterns, which is one of the reasons I have written this book in this way. Through my clients, and the resulting case studies, I have learned what I know. I have learned from being present with my clients and asking my guides constantly to teach me what is going on.*

*We are all individuals and we can never compare one person to another; although there are very many similarities* in human beings, we are also all so very different, one person's trauma is another person's lesson. One person's weirdness is another person's unique gift. For instance, unfortunately many societies raise children to believe that being wrong is a bad thing. With this knowledge, I can always use that very common belief as an opening to allow the body to connect with me and start the healing process. I also know that certain upbringings expect certain ways of being, or the pecking order of siblings often create similarities in clients who have been raised as an only child or second born or middle child, respectively. The last born child of a family of 3 kids will have a different dynamic as the last born of a family of 9 children.

A second born child who was born shortly after their older sibling will most often than not have a belief that they are a burden. This happens because most pregnant mothers who have a crawling baby or young toddler will find it a burden to have a big belly and try and keep up with their very active child. Although the mother is not actually telling the baby inside her that the baby is a burden, they do find being pregnant whilst looking after a young child to be a burden. So it's safe to say that a client who has a sibling just older than them may very well have that trauma within them. All this information helps me to understand how and why a client's patterns and trauma's feel like they do. It's *like a puzzle, but what I discover is more important than working out the puzzle, I am not trying to work it all out, I am trying to feel what is no longer needed in the client's body. What I discover just allows me to accept the client even more, to understand and have openhearted, non-judgemental compassion towards the client. I believe there is no wrong in a client, just old patterns that are no longer doing what is needed and deserve to be released to the light. I work on the belief that every client is perfect, although I have not yet had a client who has killed someone, which might be a different situation all together. The average person, the normal guy or gal about town, does not have anything truly wrong with them, they are just unique.*

*I have learned that what I write down or feel in the beginning of a session may not be the work I do later on in the session on the healing couch. My guides are constantly dropping hints and messages and my brain cannot comprehend all of it, but I know that if I just trust my feeling's I will be on the right track. I also have learned to listen to my client with everything I am, not just my ears, my entire being, not just my body, but my entire self. I allow my soul and my humanity to be part of the session, I give everything. Someone once described the way I work, after they had watched me demonstrate my work in front of an audience as, and I quote: "I have never met anyone before, where it appeared* that every part of their body seemed to be trying to learn and pick up signals – like antennae!"

During my time with a client, all of me is with the client, I do not push any energy out to find things to try discover things outside. I bring all of my energy in to me, I forget the outside world, I am totally grounded and in the moment, I forget about my life, my son, my daughter, my car. Everything is dropped and I am with my client. I am waiting and listening; for the signals, the signs, and the vibration. It could come to me through feeling, through sound, through vibration in my ears, it can come through a realisation or inspiration, through the client saying something that feels out of place to me it can just arrive, or it may just be a knowing. I know instinctively that I need to move here, to move there, to stop, to wait, to speak. I just simply trust myself in the moment, and I love it, it's my weird gift.

The Base chakra relates to childhood, not just as a baby, it relates to childhood from conception to adulthood. Let's talk about the energy of the womb. Around day forty-nine of gestation the foetus' pineal gland becomes active. From this day forward the submerged child is now able to feel and connect those feelings to their soul, the baby may not be able to comprehend the total meaning in connection to the earth plane but, energetically, it is more in contact with its soul than it will be until its return to the universe at the end of its *life. This is a fresh soul in a fresh body and the connection is perfect. That said, whatever is going on with the mother and father, or whatever is going on around the mother, is going to have an effect on the baby.*

*Now, I know this will scare a lot of people to hear this, but it's not as cut and dry as that. If, for example, you have a minor car accident whilst pregnant and no one is hurt only a bit shaken up, that will not settle with the baby. It needs to be a repeated trauma over and over. If, for instance, the parents of a soon to be born baby have been so busy trying to get a new house sorted out before the baby comes and are running behind, and every day the mum is feeling overwhelmed with not being ready and every day she prays that the baby will wait, she says to the baby in her mind, 'we are not ready for you, we are not ready for you, don't come, don't come, don't come'. If she tells the baby that they are not ready for the baby, every day, an energetic message of 'you are not welcome' may be transmitted to the baby. Also, that being pregnant and getting the house ready is creating such an overwhelming feeling in the mother that that 'overwhelming' message is sent to the baby. It is thus possible that when the baby is born, it is born with that unwelcome belief already instilled in its base chakra. So from very early in the baby's life it is already projecting this belief out into the world, but mainly on to the parents. In this hypothetical case, these could be the kind of beliefs that could have been created: I overwhelm my parents, I am unwanted, I am a burden, it is all my fault, I am not welcome. Physical things are more important than me, etc.*

## ON THE HEALING COUCH

My first connection with Alex, physically, was my right hand on his left shoulder and my left hand on his left hip joint. At that point, all I kept getting was a picture of Alex's mother, but I waited to see what other sensations I might feel before reacting to this.

*I accessed the base chakra through the hip and I waited to feel the suction on the energy in my left hand, and it helped me a great deal to make a connection with my right hand on the shoulder joint, the point of expectation. I allowed a connection to run from one hand to the other hand so that I was in flow with the client's energy as well as with the intent of connection to the base chakra. I believe this flowing connection helps get in touch with the client's energy and does not give the body a sense of being attacked, thus allowing the body to be more relaxed and able to open up.*

*I most enjoy connecting to the base chakra, it has a wonderful earthy feel to it and it hums so deeply. It is also the easiest to access and the easiest to affect change in. It's warm, even if it's in trauma, because all the trauma in the base chakra is from childhood, and childhood is warm and special, even if we were afraid and unhappy. It's all we know, and as children, we are happy with our lot no matter what.*

*The base chakra defines who we are in our world, it's our self-confidence, our self-awareness, our self-nurturing and it's our worthiness. It's where our deepest personality patterns reside, energetically, and it holds our primal 'cave' person point of view. It's our earthy, primal sexuality and our humanity, aggressively seeking to fill our deepest needs. It makes me sad that so few of us actually ever cognitively spend time really connecting to that part of ourselves, so many of us have patterns where we get so lost in our minds that we forget there is anything else for us to connect to.*

*Right then and there, with Alex, I was in the zone, 100% of me was in a holding pattern, a pattern of waiting openly to hear his body communicate with me. The act of waiting creates movement, it is a space of emptiness, and the universe needs to create a space of harmony and as such, must fill the space with what it requires to be in line with the universal laws of balance (yin and yang). So the universe must fill the space of emptiness and create a place of harmony. Waiting is exactly how I learned to do healing, by waiting and allowing the emptiness to become something and then trusting myself and learning from it. In the waiting, I felt a clear message and I felt a need to ask Alex's mum a question becoming louder and stronger, and I could not hesitate any longer.*

I could not wait any longer, so I kept my connection open with Alex and ask his mum, "What was happening for you when you were pregnant with Alex"? She said that the pregnancy seemed normal until the last few weeks. Alex was very late and small, the doctors where saying that she must have got the dates incorrect but Alex's mum was 100% sure of the date of conception. Because of the pregnancy being so long and Alex being so small she said she was very anxious. He was eventually born 3 weeks late and when he finally did arrive, he was all wrinkly and was only 5lbs 3ozs and the nurses and midwives were tutting about why he hadn't been induced earlier. She said she felt patronised by the doctors and unheard. Alex was born with his umbilical cord wrapped around his neck three times and thus had been restricting his movements and was causing him to be starved of nutrients.

Energy thudded through my body, interaction from my guide, and the realisation that I was right about the bullying, he was bullied. The bullying took place in the womb, by his umbilical cord, not only had it cut off his nutrient supply it had cut off his movement and had focused his energy into his head, and this is why he was unable to pinpoint why he felt so powerless, with such low levels of confidence all the time, it was if he was taught to be trapped in his head by his womb trauma.

I was correct about the base chakra's energetics, as well as about the throat chakra block, at the points of self expectation.

*These energetic thuds are what teach me about my work, about healing. I recognise them as messages from the energetic body of the client. They can also be as physical as hitting the underside of my hand whilst my hand is on the client, the hit can cause my hand to lifts off the client like its being ejected. These releases can manifest in a huge cathartic release, through me, or a simple little uncontrollable jerk in the client's body. It can just be a gentle little shift that neither of us feel, but it's there. I constantly ask my guides, and my client's body, what that release was, what was that movement, explain that feeling, explain that movement. How can I learn from it, what does it tell me about my client, about the human healing ability, about the clients childhood, what can I learn and how will it help this client and other clients to come and also how can it heal me? I am always healing myself through my clients. Just recently I was working on a client and we were working on weight loss and the blocks around it and while I was helping her release, I was releasing for myself too. I have learned all I know about healing through remembering the energetics of the thuds of the releases and waiting for my guides to help me explain what they mean.*

*I often wonder how the ancient Chinese created acupuncture? I think it was similar to how I am learning about healing, through years of waiting, watching, concluding and then reinforcing that over and over again for hundreds of years. I think you will notice that I use waiting often through this book, and that's because it's so very important, it's the essence of meditation, tai chi, yoga and life. As I mentioned above, to open a space and wait, creates movement. I believe it is life, all our cells are busy waiting, being themselves.*

*Bullying usually affects the sacral chakra mainly because it is a trauma affecting flight, fight or freeze responses in the body. But with this client, because all the bullying happened before birth, in the womb, it manifested as a base chakra issue.*

*The bullying, and most likely the energetic traces from being throttled by his umbilical cord, caused the block in Alex's throat chakra. Bullying always affects the throat chakra and the sacral chakra as, usually, people who are bullied may not cry out for help, but if they do, a lot of the time, for various reasons, their voices go unheard. In this case, however, it's hard to say exactly why Alex's throat chakra was affected other than perhaps self-bulling, which leads me to the self expectation points on the back of the shoulders. I was aware of the huge amounts of energy held in these points, in Alex's body. This was due to the constant pressure my client had been putting on himself, the constant self belittling and anger he had towards himself. If I release the blockages properly, after the session the client usually feels light headed and experiences a general feeling of light-ness/ liberation.*

*Self-expectation points and expectation points are ener-getic positions on our shoulders, I use these points con-stantly when working with various clients. A client who has huge amounts of expectation put on them, through childhood experiences, will often have shoulders that slump forward or have shoulder pain or neck pain. This is because the ex-pectation points on the front of the shoulders hold the energy of expectations placed upon us, the expectation points at the back of the shoulder are self expectations, these usually stem from learned beliefs and behaviour, in connection with the expectation put on us by our childhood experiences, but are increased with the persons own self-criticism and scepticism.*

*Self-expectation points that are in trauma, make people feel like they have the world on their shoulders, they are usually easily overwhelmed, they do not feel they are good enough to cope in many situations, they feel it is their responsibility to make everyone else happy. For them, keeping everyone else happy means that they prevent the chance of wronging themselves if others are not in a perceived state of happiness. This keeps them safe from the total annihilation of their confidence, because they are so certain they are responsible for everyone else's happiness.*

*The knowledge of these energetic points helps me to clear them, just placing my finger on the point and caressing it slightly or pushing on it and being aware that it needs release, can make a client take a large releasing breath without them knowing why, just my awareness creates change. I find that so empowering and fantastic that simply because I have a belief about a point on the shoulder of a client, and that when I connect with that point, in that interaction, change is created for the person. Awesome.*

After having sat with this information for a few minutes and letting my understanding expand through me into Alex, I became aware that nothing will change without him realising that it was no ones fault that he was bullied in the womb. I am aware I have only my intuition to base this on, but he chose to be with me in the session, and the connection was so good and clear that it was worth telling him my belief. I thought it was justifiable with common sense and would be strong enough to release his mind and beliefs over blaming himself for everything. It could be the direct route to a new beginning for him, no matter if I was right or wrong.

*Often the best way to help a client to heal is to just explain where I believe the issue came from. In our lives we do not realise what we learned and where we learned the behaviours that we have.*

*It's important to realise that when we were little babies, toddlers, young children we were learning everything we needed to know about life from our parents, we learned these patterns not only from watching and seeing our parents and siblings and families behave, but we also learned them energetically, in our sleep just from the feeling of the energetics in our home or vicinity. Just because we were babies didn't not mean our soul's could not learn, it did not mean our chakras were not working even better than that of our parents. During this time of life, especially as babies, we learned how to perform the basic behaviours of our lives, like how to treat partners, how mums treat daughters, how daughters treat mums, how dads treat daughters or sons,* and how sons and daughters treat dads, we learn about love and intimacy in relationships.

A couple, who made love during the night, get woken up in the morning by their young child, who jumps into bed with them. The energetics of the love making is still in the room and the child picks up the energetics of what love making is about between parents, the child will not understand this yet, and it may be 15 years or more before the child experiences these same feelings, but the energetic memory will have been created, and the child will automatically follow what it has learned from its parents.

I am very aware of this as I have seen it in myself, as well as in clients. So many of our patterns are learned energetic behaviour before we could even speak and communicate properly.

When my son, Harry, was 18 months old, his mum and I were arguing and he came in and said, 'Mummy and Daddy arguing". He knew these words because we had often told him that mums and dads argue but it's not his fault and that mum and dad love him. We realised that we must not argue as much in front of him anymore. So a week later we were in the same energetics of an argument, but were holding our tongues, waiting for Harry to go to sleep, before *we had a go at each other. Harry walks into the room we were in, he looks at us both and comfortably says "Mummy and Daddy arguing". We had not said a word, but he understood the energetics between us, he knew it was the same as when we argue. He knew energetically what was happening between us. I just want to add that, to some extent, it is good for parents to argue in front of their children, we need to teach our children that arguing is just passionate communication and hopefully leads to better understanding and making up. In this way we teach our children to deal with trauma and how to stand up for themselves and to deal with rejection.*

I looked at Alex and said to him; "I believe that you were bullied in the womb, I think that every time you moved in the womb you strangled your air and nutrient supply. Imagine what is happening for a baby in the womb over the last few weeks of its gestation, it is cramped and kicking and moving and becoming extremely confident in it's surrounding, it is feeling stronger and is getting loads of attention because it's bigger and their mum and dad can feel them. Excitement about the birth is growing and the thoughts of actually meeting their baby are frequent. But, I explained to Alex, with him, every time he moved, he bullied and hurt himself. His mum and dad were concerned for him and those were the energetics he would've picked up. He would have learned, energetically, that there was something wrong with him and he had the physical symptoms, as well as the energetic worry from his parents, he was being strangled and bullied by his umbilical cord. He was born bullied!!

I told him that I believed, and still believe, that a baby in the womb is extremely energetically aware, more aware than any other time on the earth plane, and that what happens to you in the womb, can cause huge affect on your life, especially something as traumatic as what happened to him, because it had energetic and physical realities.

So this was a life path occurrence that "happened to you" not because you or anyone else has made a mistake or been wrong. No one is to blame for this!

HE WAS NOT TO BLAME FOR THIS!!

I waited for this to sink in to his mind. I was aware that I must hold the space for him energetically, I must be 100% certain of this or his energetics would not accept it. This was easy for me since I was 100% positive that I was right about this, and I think his mum understood it to.

I then asked Alex, "so is it your fault that this happened?"

He immediately replied "no" (speed of his reply is very relevant)

I asked "whose fault it is?"

He said "no ones, it's just what happened!"

I held him energetically, meeting the understanding and energy shift in him, as his body released the belief that it was all his fault. I was prompted by my guides to click my fingers near his ear.   So I clicked them, CLICK.

*The questions were important, as was the speed at which he answered. I use this technique to release program-ing in the brain, by giving it a learning experience, rather than a blind belief. He had blamed himself for such a long time, but after the session, he had a very plausible theory of why he had had such a tough time, and the beliefs in his body started shifting and changing. He then had a far bet-ter, more positive, story in his mind to explain to himself, where he was not the 'baddy', where he was not to blame.*

*Asking him direct questions and getting such quick an-swers told me that the belief had changed so, as per the guidance from my guides, I clicked my finger to startle his brain so that it accepted the new belief, like a snapshot from a camera. The new belief gets embedded in the mind through the shock of the click, bang or loud noise, as long as the body reacts to it. I click my fingers and bang, or tap, a client's forehead often during my work. It has proven to be a powerful tool in helping the mind to accept change. Interestingly, I was working with a client from Singapore who has had many healing session from the Singaporean healers. He told me that the healers in his country also use clicking their fingers as a tool for healing in their healing sessions.*

I could feel the energetics in the room change; I could hear the frequency in the room change and was aware that this was only the first step; he still had a lot of beliefs to work through.

I connected to his base chakra, more deeply, and asked him my questions to get his subconscious to open the energetics to his time in the womb.

I asked, "Where were you born?"

He gave me the name of the local hospital and I felt the energetics open up in his base chakra.

I asked, "How old were you when you were born?"

He stays silent trying to work out the question, my hand starts to vibrate intensely as his chakra releases trauma into my hand and I begin to pull on it.

I asked, "Were you happy to be born? "

He answered, yes, and by this time, the chakra vent was at full size and I was pulling on the trauma, the vibration in my hand stopped as the trauma from the womb was released. It was such a big release that it actually took my breath away and Alex sobbed and sobbed, his mum said after she never heard anyone sob like that in her life before, but she knew it was so very necessary for Alex to release this.

*Working on a client's energy in the womb had been something I had been working on for a few months before I came to understand the right questions to ask. My guide had been making me ask client's places of birth, but I could not bring myself to understand or ask my clients how old they were when they were born. Then, one day, it slipped out before I could catch it, and I could feel the energy open up, all of a sudden I was aware of the energetics deep in the base chakra, deep down to the spine. This point, I believe, is the deepest point of energetics in the base chakra, and it was that perfect question that got me there. I use these questions, or varieties thereof, with many clients; it's been a key to me helping people who no one else has been able to help.*

*I often get energy shifts in my body or feel the feelings from clients, I can be choking violently as I release built up trauma from a client. A client will arrive and my ears will start itching or hurting, and the client will be able to relate to that, or I am told by a client that it's my left leg that is hurting, but I feel it in my right leg and, through this, I know that the clients real issue is their right leg, but their left leg has been compensating.*

*When I am working, everything that is not me, is the client. To help me be more specific, it's important for me to get to know my own body's energy feels. To get to know myself, I work on my own healing, I meditate into my chakras, I listen to my guides and I do as much inner child work as I can.*

*I work on emptying myself out so that I have space for more energy in me. When I say 'empty myself out', what I mean is, I face and deal with my greatest traumas and submit to them and release them, I have no fear of being wrong. Actually, I relish it, it's a nice feeling when you have been wrong and you then discover what is right. It's better than being right all the time; it shows me my personal, internal growth.*

I immediately moved on to releasing parent trauma, with Alex, although I did not believe that there was much, but its always worth checking. I asked for his:

- Mother's name
- Earliest memory of mother

- Father's name
- Earliest memory of father.

He answered each name easily but struggled with remembering earliest memories of his parents. It was not important to me that Alex remembered his earliest memories or not, it was a subconscious connection that I was looking for. The body and soul were aware of what I was doing, and that I was doing it for the highest of good.

*We all have different energies and upbringings which create unique relationships with every one we know. We project our energy and beliefs on to them and they project their energy and beliefs on us. These projections create a unique bond between us. Because of these unique bonds, it's important for me to get the most accurate connection with the important relationships in a client's life. Family connections are almost always the most powerful and can create the most traumas in us from our childhood. So asking questions about parents, that trigger subconscious answers in the body and chakras, allows me to get that unique individual trauma released from a client. The questions go much deeper than just the general, "how was your relationship with your parents?" Or, what was your childhood like?*

*This reminds me of a client that came to me because he was being bullied at work. He told me that his childhood was good. I was surprised because he presented energetics of being bullied, and I could feel he held tremendous trauma in his sacral chakra. I asked him if he was sure his childhood was good, and he said he had enjoyed a fabulous childhood. I asked him how he would be punished if he did something wrong. His face changed, he became anxious, and told me his father would beat him and then ignore him for days, sometimes weeks. I asked him what kind of things would result in him receiving that extent of punishment, and he said, "Anything, my father could be very irrational". So as a child he had learned to stay away from his dad, do his own thing, abiding by the family rules perfectly so he did not trigger his dad's anger, he grew up in constant trauma. Since this trauma started when he was very young, it did not feel like trauma, it was his normal modus operandi, even though he wore it like an outfit that I could see as clear as day, and could be felt by other people. People who have no awareness would just assume he needs to be bullied; he projected the expectation of getting into trouble and being bullied because it was a learned behaviour in his childhood. This is why he was getting bullied at work.*

*The most outstanding energetic he carried around was the expectation of getting into trouble. With this expectation released, and his changed projection, his bullying at work would stop. In this case, he quite quickly stood up for himself and ended up changing jobs because he realised he was not being treated how he wanted to be treated and made changes for his own best interest.*

I moved on to Alex's solar plexus and connected with his rib cage using my left hand and waited for the connection from his body. I connected with my right hand to his shoulder. I began to uncontrollably rub and tap his shoulder, I am not sure if its rub or tap, as it's so automatic for me, there is no possible way that I am actually in control of the movements, they are too quick for my brain to process. It had to be controlled by my guides and was creating a pumping release of energetics through Alex's meridian lines.

*When I connect to a client, I almost immediately seek out bone. As most of our deepest trauma has happened when we were growing up, it's obvious that as our bones grew accepting the trauma into their cells. The system of tapping bone, connecting to bone, and being with it, I believe, releases, or gives the bone a chance to change and clear, its childhood energy. I am most likely to have one hand touching neck, head, shoulder, hip or rib bones. I often work on hands, feet and knees, connecting through touch and awareness to the bones of the body.*

*In a client who has previously done work with other healers, therapists or by themselves, when I connect with bone, there can be an incredibly strong, almost instant, release and relaxation in the client. So many clients come to me as the last resort, they have been seeing a therapist or a psychologist, sometimes for years, and nothing has changed. Now, please do not get me wrong, I believe in most therapies, but some of the psychological therapies work very much on the client as an adult and in their minds. I believe the mind is 2% of a person's true self and the body or gut mind is the other 98%. So if the client has been to a psychologist or clinical therapist, there is a very good chance that they have not, what I call, downloaded the mind changes into the body. So the changes have happened in the 2% mind but have not been properly downloaded into the 98% body. I do not take the credit for these changes if they happen. Rather, I explain to the client that they have done the work, but I am going to help it to actually take affect, by connecting their mind to their body, and allowing them to work more in harmony. So when I connect to a client's solar plexus, and the client has worked on himself or herself, both the client and I usually get this successful release feeling, an uncontrolled deep breath and the automatic aaaaaaahhhhhhh feeling when you exhale and you know something has changed. Amazingly, sometimes the biggest releases just come from me being present with the client in a total accepting way; this is a core part of my healing method.*

I asked Alex to repeat sentences over and over again until I told him to take a deep breath and release the trauma.

I asked him to repeat, "It's all my fault".

As he began, I could immediately feel it reacting in the chakra and I began to pull on the feeling as he repeated this. After several times of repetition, I could feel the energy release from his chakra and I recognised that this was only a part of the release needed. I know from experience that this meant that the belief was held in a younger energy. So I change the wording. I ask him to rather repeat, " it's me". He starts to repeat 'it's me, it's me, it's me' and already I was through and I changed the sentence again to, 'me'. "Me, me, me, me', after five or six repeats, the energy was free, and I pulled it out and pushed it away. Stopping, I held energy to his chakra, so it could balance out after the release. I was aware that the shifts had been really large and I shouldn't do too much more as it would have given him an undesirable energy hangover, or unpleasant reaction, and that would've been counter productive.

I told Alex and his mum that it was enough for one session and I suggested another session in one weeks time so that we could recap and see what results we had achieved so far, and also because I had stopped to keep him safe but that there was still more to do.

I asked him if he had understood what I was doing and if he had felt that it was worthwhile coming to see me.

*Let me explain this method that I use with almost every client. I ask clients to repeat out loud negative or non helpful beliefs they may have in their bodies. Now, if I am wrong, there is no response from the body. But, if I am right, and the belief is there, the belief will energetically react because, as the person repeats the belief, it is triggered through saying and hearing the belief.*

*Hearing the belief is an acknowledgement of the belief, and thus there is an energetic and physical reaction to the belief, acknowledgment of the belief creates awareness. Awareness creates change.*

*Through hearing and acknowledging the belief, the brain is recognising the belief, which in turn, created an energetic response. This response is what I am able to connect too, it is like I have pressed a button on the specific belief and its shot up in their body and said, "Hello, here I am".*

*When we get to this point of the belief being triggered, it is up to me to know which chakra to be in when the belief is lifting, and be ready and aware enough to receive the belief in my left hand, to release it.*

*I then get the client to be active in the release of their belief by helping the release. As I feel the belief release into my hand, I ask the client to take a deep breath in and release the belief on the out breath. This interaction with the client helps to create a much more powerful release because their entire body is involved while they are focusing on their breath to release the trauma. Their minds awareness of the belief, whether they believe it or not, and the connection with me also repeating the belief in my mind with them, creates a powerful release. It's making the client take responsibility for his or her own energetics which is exactly what I want to happen - we are creating a connection to self for the client. Basically we are releasing the belief, physically, mentally, energetically and on a soul level.*

*A regular client will get used to this, and the breath of release will come totally naturally and some can even tell how deep or big the belief was that was released.*

*Only on a very few occasions have I had to work with the same belief around the same issue more than once. The most common reason for this is a client who reacts to the belief dramatically, for instance: I asked a client to release, "My mother is always right, even if she is wrong". A very common belief to release from people whose parents never listened to their child's needs, and ignored what the child has said, and were very strict.*

*I learned this from a lady client who I asked to repeat this sentence, by the end of the third repetition she was crying with huge, deep, dramatic breaths trying to contain the traumatic release, tears running, bright red face and extreme emotions. But in my hands, there was nothing, no energetic change, no shift at all. It took a while for me to work out that this client was thinking their emotions rather than feeling them and was replacing the true connection to the feelings with drama, something they may have done as a child to get attention and to distract from their true feelings of hurt and disconnection. I asked that same client the following week to repeat this belief with me this time, but without thinking, to just say the words without relating them to her life, and to say them like a mantra. She repeated "my mother is always right, even if she is wrong; my mother is always right, even if she is wrong; my mother is always right even if she is wrong". There was no dramatic emotional response, then, there was a look on her face, a look of realisation as she could feel the energetics in her sacral chakra begin to move. After the breath she said, "Ok, now that was WOW!". Then I explained to her that she had been using the drama to stay away from the actual emotions. I asked her how she felt about truly releasing and she said it was so freeing and she could feel how it had made space within her life. This method has proved itself over and over again. I have even used this on myself and tested the same beliefs on a client over a few weeks, to see if the beliefs come back and they have not.*

*I can also do this method without the client repeating the words, and I do make sure I do silent releases with every client. I find that a client who thinks a lot about the session afterwards can reprogram the belief back in their own body, so if I do a silent release every few releases, then they do not have all the knowledge to reprogram themselves.*

*I can do the same belief more than once. While working on a client's illness that is due to stress, stress related to mother, father, work and siblings can also be worked on. You may have to do releases like, "I am not good enough for mother", and a week later, "I am not good enough for father". There are many common beliefs I use over again. Things like: I am bad, I am naughty, it is not safe to change. I am never right. I am unacceptable, I am a sinner, sex is bad, sex is a weapon, and everyone is better than me; I could go on for ages with this.*

*But there are beliefs that are very interesting too, things like a person who believes both that being bad is good and being bad is bad - a vibrational energy level with opposing beliefs. These people have been told off when they are bad, so bad is bad, but they get attention when they are bad, so bad is good. Even being good can be bad; even if I have been good I get into trouble or I don't get any attention when I am being good because being good is expected always. And being good is good because I get praised when I am good. Most clients have something like this going on from childhood.*

*I believe the left hand receives energy by sending out subtle energy, as it reads and/or absorbs energy, and I believe the right hand is the flame thrower of energy as it releases power from the body. This is why healers believe they have a more powerful hand. Both sides release energy, but the left releases energy so gently and subtly that it is able to read energetics it is connecting to far more specifically, like a radar.*

*I could easily teach this way of healing to people, but I cannot teach the understanding and ability to read these subtle differences between hands, and to be able to read the client's body through this, I believe, is only something expe-*

*rience can teach. I have thousands of clients worth of expe-rience and have learned how to assess what the client's body is saying, and can assume the beliefs in their body from the information I receive from them orally and energet-ically in the beginning of the session, but, when I am pulling the first or second belief out of a chakra, and the body un-derstands what I am doing and starts to communicate with their energetic body, then all of a sudden I am in the flow and the body is throwing beliefs that it no longer wants at me. I have belief after belief shooting into my head and I am releasing two, three and four at a time, without even trying. This is when I am really helping a client, when their body is now taking over the session, communicating with me at speeds that are hard to understand and conceive of, and my guides have taken over, because I am no longer able to be the processor of the work since the vibration is too high for me to understand. Hence "Healing for the highest of good beyond my understanding""*.

Alex said he thought he understood it all and was very happy he came to see me and that he would be back next week. He asked me why he had to repeat the negatives of his beliefs. I responded to him saying that we wanted to activate the belief, so we repeated it out loud so the brain was saying it, hearing it and therefore must acknowledge the belief. Acknowledgment creates awareness, awareness creates change and through that, the body energy reacts to the beliefs because we have activated the energetics of the beliefs, and I can then grab hold of them and pull them out.

We made a follow-up appointment and I took payment from his mum (I do not like this as it is not a full exchange from the client themselves, but I could not complain since the session was very productive and should settle).

They leave.

My feeling after they left was that of joy. I know the feeling of a very successful session and I knew this one was very successful. What is more important is that I confirmed for myself that my theory about how the energetics of the experience of being in the womb can, and does, affect us as we grow older. Over the next few weeks I learned to define this as 'SC', Submerged Child, as an addition to the transactional analysis trio of Parent, Adult and child, in the typical break down of the human psyche.

## TESTIMONIAL

*The following is a testimonial from Alex;*
**Alex's Testimonial**

I first went to see Wayne Lee when I was 23, at a time

when I was going through something of a breakdown. Even though there wasn't any major trauma that I was aware of, it was stopping me from living my life to its full potential; I was falling apart. I felt emotionally disconnected from my life and those around me, and this filled me with huge feelings of unhappiness and guilt.

Being spiritually minded souls, my mum and auntie encouraged me to seek healing and my mum arranged for me to see Wayne. I must admit I was somewhat sceptical before first seeing him, but I will never forget that first session. Through the guidance he received, Wayne pinpointed a profound trauma I was able to release; one that neither my mum nor I was aware was affecting me in such a huge way. It stemmed from the cord being wrapped around my neck at birth – the trauma on the moment of coming into the world, which had stayed with me subconsciously since, and was now asking to be resolved.

I still remember the enormous weight which was lifted from me at that moment, when Wayne first pinpointed that subconscious trauma and allowed it to be released. I remember the profound feeling of peace which followed, something which I couldn't remember feeling in such a deep way before that. I now believe that those experiences that happened to me at birth, happened in order that my experience of healing should be so deep, beautiful and totally life-changing.

In the year that followed, while still seeing Wayne regularly, I sought healing and spiritual realisation in many aspects of my life. I also began my own journey as a healer and I hope in the future I may be able to help others in even a fraction of the way that Wayne helped me. His abilities are truly extraordinary – literally miraculous.

I am now engaged with two small children and I know that without Wayne I could never have experienced the happiness and contentment I am now blessed with. I owe him and the loving spirits that work through him the most profound gratitude.

# Sarah and her Feminine Feathers

*(Name has been changed to protect Sarah's identity)*

## Overview

In this case study we explore how our beliefs create our reality and that our patterns and traumas can come from beyond this life and how past lives can play a part in who we are in our lives now.

We also explore the power of distant healing and how the "unbelievable" can become our reality and sometimes just the ramblings of an intuitive healer can change our worlds for the positive.

Sarah's journey to be allergy free, to be able to live her life her way, in her power, and have no guilt to hold her back, combined with the wonders of how her choice to follow a path of self healing, has given her more than she could ever have imagined.

# INTRODUCTION

Sarah is a client who had been to see me for at least five sessions, successfully working towards changing different aspects of her life. I would like to mention two of the changes that Sarah and I worked on over the time she asked me for help.

Often with clients it's just the little breakthroughs that allow them to believe in the ability for them to heal and to trust that I can help them with their healing. I do not believe we had any major breakthrough sessions in the first four or five sessions. What we did have, though, was the opening of her awareness. She was seeing how her beliefs could be affecting her life. I think she trusted my gentle communications of the detailed understanding that I had of how her beliefs and patterns could be affecting her.

As I write this, I become aware of how she felt to me in those sessions, and more importantly, how the way she felt changed through those sessions. I think the best way for me to describe it is my awareness of a sense of balance in self-acceptance and confidence that was growing progressively within her, session by session. This allowed Sarah to be open to change, so if I suggested something different to help her, she was open and willing to listen and she trusted me to go for it no matter how bizarre or different it was to her normal thinking.

*What makes me unique is that I am not afraid to go out of the normal and into the completely unusual, wacky, way out there, darned impossible. My obsession to be without boundaries in the healing progress is balanced out by the almost perfect time- keeping and structure I like to have whilst I am working. I like very much to have everything as symmetrical as possible when I connect to my client on the healing couch. If a piece of clothing is laying out of place, I need to straighten it and if there is a crumb or hair on the person's clothing then I need that removed too. This actually makes me giggle at myself. I am about to enter a person's energy and body with my mind and soul and I am worried about the hair that is stuck to their sweater! Not just worried, it truly bothers me and more often than not I'll have to remove the obstruction or ask the client to remove it for me.* ☺

## CLIENT INFO

Sarah is a 32 year old British woman. She is tall and attractive with a very well-groomed look.  Sarah is self-aware and willing to work on herself without fear of dealing with her personal issues. She knows it is better to seek harmony rather than happiness. She comes from a caring, if headstrong family (I wondered if the family was over-caring and more controlling). She does struggle with a poor image of herself at times and can get stuck in that pattern blindly.

## ONE

The first change I will mention is to do with Sarah's male and female energetic balance without going into too much personal detail.

I was working with Sarah on clearing issues she had about her femininity. Sarah's upbringing had instilled in her fears that being a woman is not always safe and feminine attributes, like curvy hips and breasts, were just going to make her a target for men to scorn and ridicule. In the session we went about removing these beliefs. We released beliefs from her childhood like:

- *"I am not safe being a girl/woman."*
- *"Women are only for sex."*
- *"Men use women."*
- *"Women are for men to use."*
- *"It's better being a man."*
- *"Being a woman is bad."*

- *"Men are better than women." etc...*

Whilst I was doing these releases I was very aware of her female energy shifting. I could feel the movement of energy from the left to the right of her body. This meant, to me, that there was a very strong balancing of Sarah's energy in the male-female energy level. As I held the space for Sarah I was shown intuitive images of Sarah with a much fuller chest. This triggered thoughts and ideas and I found myself telling Sarah that there is a chance that these shifts we had been making, I believed, were unblocking female energy and could cause hormonal changes to occur. These hormonal changes would be a balancing of her original hormone balance which was created when she was a teenager, the same one that held all those feminine fears and negative belittling beliefs.

She asked me what that meant for her. I said that there was a small chance that she may have a change to her breast size as her body may allow an increase in the amount of female hormones to flow, compared with what her belittling beliefs had allowed. Sarah smiled and said she would be happy to have an increase in her breast size. I told her that there was no guarantee that this **would** happen, but I had been shown by my guides that this may be the case and she could expect, if I was right, an increase of up to two cup sizes. I told her I had heard of this being done through hypnosis, so I knew it was possible.

Our session came to an end and Sarah left feeling really balanced and, I think, a little sceptical. I was excited to see what the outcome would be. What the change would be, if any.

## FEEDBACK

Six weeks later I saw Sarah for her next session. She told me that the month after her last session, she had an increasing sensitivity and slight pain in her breasts and had actually ended up growing one full cup size. She said that she was amazed at how quickly it had worked and how sensitive and painful her breast had gotten. She was also very happy and amazed at the changes.

She was content with this and was worried that her breasts may keep growing. I assured her that I thought it had stopped because she had not had any sensitivity or pain for two weeks and she should not worry about any more gain. We then continued with her session.

*What I ended up doing with Sarah was creating a balancing in her male-female energetics. This is, in my opinion, a third eye chakra energy balancing. I believe the third eye balances out the energetics between the left and right of the brain.*

*The left hemisphere of the brain is masculine, (reasoning, outgoing energy) and controls the right side of the body. The right hemisphere of the brain is feminine, (creativity, in-coming energy) and controls the left side of the body. The third eye chakra is the balance of these hemispheres.*

*If you are extremely creative (right brain) and cannot reason or express that creativity (left brain) the creativity is then stuck, we need to be more balanced for us to be in flow with our creativity. For instance, inspiration is a mixture of intuition (right brain) and reason (left brain). The ability to receive information and then process this information comes from communication from right brain to left brain and left brain to right brain. The communication portal that controls this is the third eye chakra or pineal gland.*

*If one side of a client's energy brain is drastically weaker than the other, I find this is caused from childhood trauma that is held in the client's beliefs of what is acceptable or not for that client, in accordance to their upbringing. This childhood trauma, I have found, usually stems from too much unexpressed expectation put on a child from parents who may not communicate openly with the child but still expect certain manners or behaviour from the child and then blame the child for not fulfilling the adult's unspoken expectations. As you address this energy, and balance it out, clients enter into more of a male-female harmony within themselves.*

*So a balancing of the third eye can create large shifts of energy that can, and do, affect the physical body in many different ways. With Sarah, I believe this was a hormonal change allowing her to be more feminine in her energy, but to do this, she had to allow herself to be more masculine. Sounds confusing, but it is simple. For her to be more feminine she had to have more masculine strength to believe in her femininity.*

*I think it is important to note that, energetically, what makes a strong female is masculine energy; she is a woman, she has the genitalia, softness, curves and nurturing instincts of a woman, but it takes masculine strength to be a strong woman, to decide what is right for her and to not worry about what others think. A strong woman chooses what is right for her and makes the decisions that are most sensible and balanced in connection with her emotions and present situation, thus using her masculine energy to be a strong woman.*

*With men the process is exactly the same but with opposite energies. To be a strong man, takes feminine energy. A man is a man. He has the genitalia, muscles and strength of a man, but it takes feminine energy to make a strong man. A strong man is physically stronger and more powerful than*

*women and children but it takes the feminine energy of nur-
turing, compassion and softness to make a man complete
and strong. It is the balance of male and female energy that
creates strong individual people.*

## TWO

Sarah contacted me to ask if I could help her with an
allergy. She said that she had once again had a severe allergic reaction to feathers. She had bought a new coat that,
after a short time of wearing it, had given her a strong allergic reaction. She realised the coat had goose down feathers in the filling. She worked out that it was the goose down
feathers in the lining of the coat that had triggered her allergy. She wondered if it was possible for me to help her
clear this allergy. She also told me she had allergies to fur
and any animal hair that falls out.

My first response was to tell Sarah that I had never done
this before, but I believed there was always an energetic
reason for every physical reaction we have and, if she
wanted to, we could give it a go. We could try and discover
what energetics would be causing this allergy, and see if
we could release it. I told her I could not promise it would
work at all and that it may need 3-4 sessions for me to

discover what was needed to shift this. She agreed and we arranged a time for her session.

*I believe, and quantum physics has also proven, that at the smallest particle of everything, there is only energy: energy molecules. Scientists are trying to find anything that is actually physical and have as yet not succeeded. So at the moment, everything is first energy, then seemingly physical.*

*I believe we are a soul with a body, not a body with a soul. With this in mind, I believe that looking for what the energetic cause behind the physical manifestation of our trauma is, dis-eases, pains, physical feelings and what their symptoms are, is the first step, and then re-educating these parts of ourselves is the next step. There are many tools to re-educating our energy. We could look at the "inner child" aspect, therapy, healing, self- acceptance and simply bringing this energy into the light so it is no longer left to grow in a dark, unseen part of who we are.*

*Changing the energy that is the root cause of our pains and traumas will, if we allow it, change who we are physically, as well as emotionally. So many times I have come across clients who have had such traumatic upbringings that were either very strict or judgemental or they have learned that it is not safe for them to be different in any way because if they are, they will get into trouble, or be ridiculed, for being different or out of the expected norm. So all these clients believe it is safer to stay the same and never change. In this we find that the client can try everything possible to change, deal with illness or repetitive patterns and always get no results, no change and often make themselves worse. This is because their body has a belief that 'they are not safe to change' so the healers, doctors and therapists that have tried to help, have not got anywhere.*

*I would work to release this belief. Without this belief the body then allows change. If I describe the difference in how the client's energy feels to me, I would say that when they hold the belief and I connect to the client, it would be like I was trying to go through a brick wall. However, after the belief is released, it feels like the wall has begun crumbling and I can reach through at points. Then, every time after that when I connect, the wall has crumbled more and more. These clients usually experience quite profound stages of emotions over the next few weeks as their bodies learn to deal with allowing change, and they begin to release everything that has been held back. It is like breaking the dam wall that has been holding the client's emotions back.*

*I believe we create everything we are as we learn and established self beliefs. I have had a client who realised during our session that at five years old she had decided it was safer for her emotionally if she was responsible for her mother and now, fifty years later, she is still living with and*

*looking after her mother. First, she created the energetic be-*
*lief and then over time that belief manifested into her phys-*
*ical future and is now her actual present creation.*

*I have seen clients release decades of food allergies by*
*looking at what was happening around the dinner table*
*when they were children, and seeing what their parents be-*
*lieved and instilled in them in connection to food. Confusing*
*messages like; "You have to eat healthy or you will be fat."*
*"Here, would you like some chocolate cake?"*

*When I work on these types of beliefs I like to recreate*
*the atmosphere the client learned them in. For instance,*
*asking the client to remember the house and the dinner ta-*
*ble, or a specific event where they may have learned the*
*belief, and then allow the adult part of the client to release*
*their own trauma by bringing that confused child energy into*
*the light and accepting the actual trauma, not the physical*
*side effect. So we bypass the physical and go back under-*
*neath to find the energetic cause.*

*When working on the types of trauma that can cause al-*
*lergies, I look for what could be responsible for this energy*
*trauma from before birth all the way to the first remembered*
*onset of the allergy.*

*The following are the basic things I look for information about. With this information, I can detect the point of creation of the trauma, so I can take the client back to that point and release it through re-education or energy shift:*

- *Concept of life (why their parents conceived the person)*
- *What was happening for their mother during their pregnancy with my client?*
- *What was their birth like for mother and child?*
- *What are their siblings' ages - if any? (Did any of them have difficult births?)*
- *How were they put to sleep at night? (cried to sleep or held to sleep)*
- *Were they breast fed? (breast is most definitely best)*
- *What do they remember about eating food when they were children?*
- *Did any of their parents have eating disorders?*
- *Were there any lost children before or after their birth?*

*With all this information at hand it can help to find a direction to release what their body is holding, but some people do not know all this information, and cannot find out as parents have passed away or also do not remember. In this case, we use what we have and I will compare it with other clients and feelings and intuitions that I will be given and use that to assume what could have happened. It makes no difference if I am right or wrong because if I am wrong there will be no reaction energetically in the client's body, but if I am close or right, then their body will have an energetic reaction and we can make a shift with that. However, it is very important that when I do hypothesise that I tell the client that I am doing this. I make sure that the client does not take on any of the beliefs that I am coming up with. I am very careful with this. It's not my job or any therapist's or healer's job to add trauma to the body whilst they are working with their client. So I make sure that the client knows that I am hypothesising and, even if I am right, to not dwell on it or create stories around it.*

*At times, one area that I find difficult to deal with is when I tell a client that what they feel and believe has happened to cause trauma (and thus allergies or illness), and they immediately deny what I have discovered. Now, I am always open to being wrong because being wrong gives us a direction of how to find what is right, but often I know I am right. I know it because I recognise the energetics and I have to accept that the client either is not yet ready to accept this in their life or I am wrong and must accept that for myself.*

*Luckily enough, on most occasions, I can find the way to understand why I have felt that energy and use that to help the client. More often than not, I am right. I have to trust the energy and believe in myself. Historically I have found that trusting what I believe has worked to help many clients, no matter if I am right or wrong.*

## THE SESSION

The following day I connected with Sarah for her session. I asked Sarah whether she remembered the first time she had had a reaction to feathers. Sarah told me that when she was around four years old her mum had taken her to a farm play area, and within minutes of walking into a chicken coop, her face had swollen up and her breathing had become restricted and her mother rushed her out of the coop to get her medical assistance. Sarah told me that she knows when she is getting an allergic reaction because her hands get hot, her face starts to go red and swollen and she feels like she has got something caught in her throat, whilst her breathing becomes restricted. I mentioned to Sarah that I had had a feeling that something was in my throat for about an hour before her session and that I had been drinking water to try and clear my throat, but that it had not yet cleared and I was aware that it had something to do with her trauma.

*It is not uncommon for me to feel what needs working on, for a client, hours before their session. I remember once in London, while waiting for a client to arrive for her session, I was chatting to one of my colleagues and noticed that my behaviour was different to normal. I was jumping about and being very jittery in my manner and speech. I noted this to my colleague that this jittery behaviour was not my energy and I assured him that my new client due to arrive shortly will have some anxiety issues. Not long after this the door-bell rang and my client arrived. Once in the privacy of the therapy room I asked her why she had chosen to see me and she answered, "Because I am always so anxious"!*

*When this happens I just take note of it but do not let it stop me from living my life. A very close friend of mine had booked a session to see me one Thursday afternoon at 2pm. I woke up that morning with a headache and a slight feeling of 'flu. By 11 am I was in agony with the headache and feeling awfully ill. Medication had not helped my headache and I knew I was not fit to do a session. I called my friend and said to her that I was too ill to see her and we would have to reschedule the session. As soon as I put the phone down the headache and feelings of being ill went away and I was right as rain again in minutes. I called her back and told her either I am the wrong person to do the session or she is not ready for the healing yet. Over the next few months it became apparent that she was not yet ready to deal with what she had chosen to work on that day and later that year we did work on it with much success.*

My guides had already shown me a few things and I knew I needed to take Sarah back to the chicken coop when she was four so that I could feel the energy change in her body, to understand what happened to her, and to see if I could help her.

I asked Sarah to close her eyes and to imagine she was four years old and about to go into the coop where the feathers are. Within seconds I felt an energetic surge that felt extremely long and empty to me. At the same time, Sarah said she could not go any further. She had felt that feeling that happens when she starts to get an allergic reaction. She said it felt like her whole body was being lightly shocked by energy that seemed to shift her into an uncomfortable sensation all around her body. Sarah noted to me that she actually knew when she was going to get an allergic reaction because of this uncomfortable feeling she got, almost like a warning that she was going to have the allergic reaction.

In my mind I was seeing space and distance. I was seeing way beyond a four year olds life. I was seeing her past lives. I told Sarah I did not think that this was to do with this current life, but brought through from a previous life. Immediately Sarah agreed with me saying that that felt about right to her too. She always wondered why the feeling was so strong around this.

At this point I was surrounded by my guides and was seeing things that made sense to me, but I needed them to make sense to Sarah.

Everything I was about to talk Sarah through had already flashed through my head, with increasing clarity several times. I told Sarah what I was seeing. In a past life, I believe, she had been a petite 14 year old house maid in an old grand house during the 18th century. I told her that she was walking down a walkway on the side of a court yard near the staff quarters of the house. She got a feeling, a feeling of not being secure, a feeling she knew, a feeling of being attacked. She was then suddenly scooped up and forced into a room by a huge brute of a man, a man that smelled of animals and bad body odour. A man she had always been afraid to stand up to because he was well liked by the lord of the house as he looked after the lord's animals. He pushed her down onto an old broken feather mattress that was out of the house waiting to be repaired. He had forced her face into the broken mattress. This had

happened to her before by him but this time she had decided she was going to fight back. She was pushing up with
her hands whilst this brute of a man pushed her head
down into the broken mattress. Feathers from the mattress
were going everywhere. The harder she pushed away and
fought him, the harder he pushed her head into the feathers so she could not breathe. She tried to take a breath and
her throat filled with feathers. She started to suffocate and
as he brutalized her from behind the pressure he was putting on her head and the feathers in her throat had suffo-
cated her and she died there on that broken feather
mattress.

Sarah listened quietly and then said that that explained
the heat in her hands, from pushing back on the bed, with
the broken feathers pricking and tearing at her hands and
the closed throat from the feathers being in her throat and
the red face from her face being pushed into the rough bed.
She also said it explained many other things in her life too.

I asked Sarah if she wanted me to help clear this energy
brought through from a past life and Sarah readily agreed.

I asked her to close her eyes and to imagine this young
petite girl with her face pushed into a broken bed with
feathers everywhere. I asked her to see this young girl
fighting back by trying to push up with her hands, but that
this just makes this brute even more aggressive. I told her

that what I wanted her to be visualising was just after he had attacked her. He had just pushed her into the bed. I asked Sarah to imagine or visualise herself as she was now, walking into that room with a large heavy baseball bat and to beat the brute! Beat him hard and show the bully who was boss, and then to grab the girl and take her away from there and make her safe.

I stopped and waited, allowed the energy to settle with Sarah. I could feel energy had shifted. I could also sense from Sarah that she felt it too. We were both quiet for a moment longer.

She said to me, "Wow, that was really powerful! I could feel it. It felt so real. As I walked in the room, I could feel that uncomfortable feeling that I get when I go near feathers." She paused and then said, "It felt really good hitting him."

I sat quietly for a short while just listening to the energy and seeing whether there was anything else for me to do, but my guides and intuition were silent. It had been just under half an hour since we started the session. All we could do then was to wait and see if this helped Sarah's allergy to feathers.

I told Sarah that she must not expect any change for the next few days. Firstly, she was already recovering from her recent reaction to wearing her new coat, so suggested that she not go near the coat or feathers for 48 hours to let her body heal. Thereafter, she should just pick up the coat and see if she got that same uncomfortable feeling from it or not. I told her to follow her gut feeling and to carefully try and see if it had helped, not to go and shock her body and trigger another reaction, but to let me know over the next week.

One last thing I need to mention is that this session was done whilst I was in Bournemouth, South of the UK and Sarah was in New York, USA. We were doing the session over Skype, 5500 kilometres apart.

## FEEDBACK

This is the text message I got from Sarah, word for word, three days after the Skype session:

"Wayne Wayne Wayne, you bloody genius!! I've worn my coat for about 12 hours and I feel great! Absolutely no reaction whatsoever. You're a legend! How much do I owe you? Sarah X

Sarah has since then not needed to worry about her allergy to feathers at all. Also, I now have a regular flow of clients for Skype sessions from New York!

*It really makes very little difference to me where my client*

*is. It is all about how I work within myself and holding the space correctly within me, for my client. Distant healing sessions can be far more powerful for some energetic blocks. I have experimented extensively with clients and distant healing. I think it's the lack of barriers that the client puts up because there is no "face to face" fears or anxiety being triggered, and mostly the client is in the comfort and safety of their own home or space.*

*Distance does not exist to energy. Everything is connected energetically to each other. We have all experienced this at some point in our lives when we suddenly think of a friend and then the phone rings and it is them. We think about a friend or family member and they contact us because they had thought of us too. You know your partner is in a bad mood even before you get home. We all can make our friends and family feel love and affection over the phone. It's just the same thing when using distance healing. I am just using it a little bit more specifically and controlling the connection with energy to a much more in-depth level, focusing on healing, releasing and clearing, full of love and acceptance that you may not always get with family and friend connections.*

*When I use my intuition, I use it 100%. It gently controls me from the time I release myself to it. I trust it so intensely that the images become clearer and clearer and it makes no difference if I am right or wrong. It is not about right or wrong, it is about connecting to the issue and using any possible method to help a person move forward in their life, even if the release is from an ancestral or a past life energy. As long as I am not creating new trauma or increasing old trauma, it cannot hurt the client if my intuition is wrong.*

*Without me trusting my intuition and being courageous and open enough to express this to Sarah, she may never have got rid of this allergy, or it may have been years before Sarah found a way to release her allergy. Once again, it is an energetic trauma that created a physical reaction. However, there are times where no healer will be able to help you release a trauma, illness or allergy because that struggle is part of your life lessons and is there to teach you.*

*It is amazing how many different things could be affecting a client. With this in mind, I have begun to work with clients looking at what the actual intention of life was for them. I wonder what kind of energy is affecting a client if they were born out of wedlock years ago, when being born out of wedlock was seriously frowned upon. I wonder what kind of trauma a person has when their parents conceive them to save their marriage. I wonder what kind of trauma a person has when their mother was forced or raped during conception, or if a mother gets married and has a child to escape her parents, or trap a man. I have even come across a woman who had a baby so she could own someone that would love her unconditionally. What kind of effect do these intentions have on that child years later and how can I help clear that so that they do not take on their parents' or grand- parents' or any ancestral or past life energetics forward into their current and future lives?*

*I am constantly striving to understand more and totally love the lessons as they come to me. I hope I get the oppor- tunity to help people, and am secure in myself that I am able to help. It's my calling. It is very much who I am.*

## TESTIMONIAL

The following is a testimonial from Sarah;

"I remember meeting my Mother for lunch one day. There was a look on her face that I'd never seen before. A look of self-satisfaction and deep authentic confidence. When I asked what was going on, she told me she had just had a healing with a man called Wayne. My desire to see Wayne immediately; was overwhelming!

After my first session with Wayne I realised my life was going to be very different from then on.

Wayne and I have been on a collaborative journey for a few years now. I say collaborative because that's exactly what it is. It feels as though Wayne projects himself inside of me (in a completely un-intrusive and harmless way). He has a look around inside, sees the problem and then together, we fix it. It's always a profoundly powerful experience, every time is unique and because I feel as involved in the process as Wayne is, the problem is dealt with there and then and I have moved on from it for good.

Since my first session with Wayne, I have transformed into a confident, productive and successful woman. A woman very much evolved from the frightened, angry girl I was when we first met. I have cleared, shifted and altered my perception of myself and my reality in ways I never would have imagined. For me, a session with Wayne is a commitment to myself to realise my fullest potential as human being."

Thank you

Sarah

# Summer and the Purple Pencil Sharpener

## Overview

In this case study we explore how the unbelievable world of spirituality can, on rare occasions, affect us negatively and can bring fear and disharmony to our world, and, how being focused and fearless can be our greatest power and healer.

I explain that we are naturally safe on the earth plane and how intuition, inspiration and faith in one self can bring healing that creates change in the direction of people's lives.

Summer, who is three years old, comes to me because no one can explain why she is so poorly. After just twenty minutes of intuitive healing, and a little bit of magic, she is distracted her from the downward spiral that has been pulling her away from being the happy little girl that she is meant to be.

## BOOKING

A friend of mine called me up to ask me if I thought I could help a 3 year old girl named Summer. Summer is the daughter of a friend of his, Emma. Summer had fallen ill over the Christmas holidays and had just not recovered. Three months later, doctors had found that she had developed an ever-increasing amount of inexplicable water near her heart. My friend told me that he was not sure her mother and father would be open to bringing Summer to see someone in alternative therapies, like me, but we could only give it a go and speak with Summer's mum. Summer's parents owned, and ran, a local restaurant by the sea, and my friend and I planned to have lunch there and then approach her mum and see how she felt about it.

That very day, a Monday, we went for lunch at their restaurant and were waiting until the end of the meal to chat to Emma about her daughter. I do not know if it was luck or a guided event, but just before we spoke with Emma, Summer's baby-sitter for the day (her Granddad) brought Summer into the restaurant. I watched Summer walk through the restaurant; I began to shiver as I saw what was happening to her. I could see a lost spirit with its arm reaching into her heart. The lost spirit looked at me with venom in its eyes and I realised the shivers in me, were my guides protecting me from this vicious glare directed at me. I turned to my friend and said, "Summer is being spiritually attacked by something very nasty and she needs urgent help."

When Emma came to the table to chat, my friend explained to her what I do and I told her briefly and lightly what I thought was happening to her daughter, I did not want to scare Emma any more than she already was, as a mother with an ill daughter, but I needed her to know it was very serious. Emma surprised us by telling us that her friend who lives up north was a Reiki master and had told Emma that she too believed that Summer was being attacked. I gave Emma my card and told her to call me to book a time to bring Summer to see me.

*Please excuse my lack of memory about exactly what was medically happening with Summer, I find it very difficult to remember medical type information. I have had no training in medicine, so it slips from my mind very easily, but I remember that lost soul's face. It came across very masculine to me, but gender really is representative of humanity and I do not want to give that lost spiritual energy any humanity, it was aggressive and repulsive. Even just writing this makes me feel like retching from the thought of it, now years later.*

*I mentioned in the introduction to this book that I have*

*experienced negative responses from people when they find out what I do for a living, so walking into the restaurant to speak to Emma, I had to prepare myself to talk to a lady I did not know and telling her about my abilities, back then, it was stressful for me. Then, after seeing that lost spirit attacking her daughter, it became a situation of her believing me and trusting what I saw was real. I did not intend to convince her; I never force anyone to see me, it has to be of their own free will. If I try and convince people, the session will not work. A while ago, I had a lady try and promote me, she used neuro-linguistic programming techniques to convince people to see me, every one of those sessions did not work, they did not flow, and I was unable to connect with the client. I cannot help someone who is not willing to be there with me of their own free will. It was refreshing to know that Emma had already had the suggestion about Summer being spiritually attacked and that it had already opened the door to her believing me and allowing me to help Summer.*

## PREPARATION

In my mind, it was extremely urgent that Emma bring Summer to see me as soon as possible. Emma's reaction to my news was that of urgency too, so I was surprised and concerned when I did not receive a call to book Summer's session that day or the next. Summer stayed in my mind all week as I prepared to go away for 3 days of seeing clients in Leeds, leaving on the Friday night.

On that Friday morning I got a call from Emma, her voice had a sound of urgency to it, as she spoke to me. She told me that, after I left the restaurant on the Monday, my business card vanished, and over the next 4 days everything she did to try and contact me was blocked; her phone stopped working and her internet went down. That morning she visited a friend who happened to have my number, and she called immediately. We booked an appointment for Summer to see me that afternoon, as I was going away that evening. I was not yet sure how I would deal with the situation, so I did no preparation. I have done many spirit removals before, but none of them were actually causing such a devastating effect on a child. To me, this was on the extreme side of unacceptable and I waited in calm for them to arrive.

*I have learned through the years that some of the strangest things can happen before or during a session. I believe the lost soul was doing as much as it could to stop Emma from bringing Summer to see me. It knew I could see it, it also knew I was not afraid, and it knew that my intention was to remove it. Most often my preparation for a client is to just be open and to be at full focus, to allow myself to be aware of everything that could be going on. Often, in sessions, the slightest suggestion or energy can be a clue to making changes. Sometimes it can be frustrating that I can see what needs changing but the client is not ready to release it. What's interesting though is that that client will keep coming back to me until they are ready to release, even if I do not see them for 6 months or a year. All of a sudden, they will call me up, book to see me and we clear the problem really quickly.*

## ARRIVAL

I watched Summer and her mum arrive from my healing room window. I felt the anger and aggression towards me even before they had got out of their car, and I knew it was going to be an interesting session releasing this lost spirit attached to Summer. Summer felt totally withdrawn from life as she came towards the house, way too quiet for a 3 year old. Emma felt frazzled, with huge surges of fear and worry, the fear was thick and syrupy. I recognised that fear, I had seen it before when doing other lost spirit removals.

I know that the fear is what the lost soul is using for energy. I brought them into the house and got them comfortable in my healing room. Summer sat on her mum's knee.

## BASIC INFO

Summer is a 3 year old girl.

She lives locally with her parents and siblings and is usually a vibrant outgoing child.

## REASON FOR CLIENT SEEING ME

Last year, around Christmas, Summer caught a virus and had become quite severely ill. Emma told me that they had been really worried about her health during that illness. As she slowly recovered from the illness, her 3 year old zest for life just never returned. After a few months, Emma took Summer to the doctor; they did some more research, and discovered water collecting around her heart that they felt was causing her to be so low in energy. They had been treating her but with very little change to Summer's well-being.

## My First Assessment

Although I have already given you my first assessment of Summer when I saw her in the restaurant, I have more to add. When she was in my healing room I realises that it was not only Summer that I had to work on that day, I had to distract the energy around Emma, and I needed to break the chain of energy that was feeding this lost soul.

I could also see that Summer had protected herself really well; she had withdrawn her soul energy by pulling it to one side and was trying her best to keep her energy away from the attacking lost soul. I could see that Summer's soul was aware that something was not right, and that by protecting itself, in turn it was protecting Summer.

*When Summer was really poorly before Christmas, she dropped her natural protection, and the lost soul entered her body. Consequently, she rapidly lost power and had to push her soul to the side to protect herself as best as she could. But, seeing as though she was so poorly, her parents, and grandparents began to worry and were fearful and this fed energy to the lost soul. It's obvious the more ill she became, the more the family would worry and be fearful and the more power was available for the lost soul.*

*For a lost soul to possess someone, they need to be able to bypass the person's natural protection, a protection that we are all born with, and to do that, they need either per-mission from that person, or the person needs to lose total control of themselves through drug use, alcohol use, being knocked out or under a forced state of unconsciousness (general anesthetic, but this is extremely rare because the people doing the operation are focusing on the wellbeing of the person and in turn creating a protection for them). Then we need to feed that lost soul our energy and allow it to have power over us. This can happen to anyone. It is not some-thing we are used to dealing with, so when it happens, it can affect the strongest of us. It only takes fear and uncer-tainty to allow a lost soul to have power over us. Although in my experience with adults, this is more likely to happen to people who have large insecurity issues.*

*Focused energy, like anger or passion, is not energy that can feed spirit attachments. It is directed and has intention behind it. What can, and does, feed attached spirits is the energy of confusion, uncertainty, self-doubt and most of all, worry and fear. Fear and worry are not focused, they are just released energies that ooze out of the body and are free to be used at the spirit attachment's will. An example of this; I had been called and asked if I could help with a spirit re-moval. It was local to me, so I got into my car and went straight over. When I arrived, I was escorted up the stairs to a largish bedroom. There I found a 17-year old young woman on a bed, strapped by her hands to the metal head-board, like a scene from an old horror movie. She was writh-ing around aggressively and a type of unnatural roar came out from under her breath. Next to the bed was a line of chairs with the young woman's mother, grandmother, aunt, father and a spiritual medium. Standing next to the bed was a priest, who seemed to be shaking in his boots. With the chairs next to the bed it felt like a spectators sport.*

*All I could see was a room full of fear. Mum's fear, dad's fear, grandmother's fear, everyone was feeding fear and worry into the room. Being my usual self, I rolled my eyes at the situation and said, "Would you like me to help you with this situation?" I got an uncertain consent; yes. I said, "Right, if you want to help me help her, I need you all to go downstairs to the kitchen, start making us all a cup of tea and while you are doing the tea, I want you to all sing silent night three times". (Silent night was just the first song that came into my head, it really does not matter what they were going to do, as long as it was making them focus on some-thing else, even if that something else is thinking that I was a total nutter).*

*As they left the room, I focused calmly on the young lady. I asked her if she wanted me to help her, she nodded her head. She had stopped writhing by this time and was calm, all the fear from her family was gone - it went downstairs to make tea with them, and all there was in the room was my focus and calmness and the echo of silent night being sung badly from downstairs. I spoke to the lost soul in her and said, "Do you see me?" I said, "Look at me and see I have no fear! Look at me and see my guides". I then simply reached into her with my mind and made a way out for the lost soul and pushed it into a bright light that I had arranged my guides to open for me. I untied her and we went downstairs for tea.*

*If you stop providing the fuelling energy that the lost soul needs, it loses all its power and has no strength to fight you anymore. It's not always that easy, but it will give you an idea of what my intention was with Summer, as your read further.*

## THE SESSION

I could see Summer was feeling scared, but I also knew that she was projecting more of her mother's fears than her own. I knew that I could not get rid of this attachment without first distracting Emma. I started by just edging forward to where Summer was sitting on her mum's lap, I put my hands out and allowed myself to connect lightly with Summer's energy.

The attachment roared at me with more power than it should have. I knew that I could not release the attachment without first blocking the energy that was fuelling it. I looked around the room for something that I could use to distract Summer and Emma, what I found was a purple pencil sharpener. The purple pencil sharpener came with a pack of colouring-in pencils I had bought from a local retailer (I use the colour pencils for teaching Reiki level 2 and for drawing pictures of energy and chakras, I have around 10 sets of pencils and sharpeners).

I showed the purple pencil sharpener to Summer and Emma and with a quick slight of hand, I made the purple pencil sharpener disappear; I moved closer to summer and pulled the purple pencil sharpener out of her ear. (Slight of hand and magic has always been something I have enjoyed learning). I used this distraction technique 3 or 4 times to get Emma's and Summer's attention and as I did it, I was able to put a hand on and off of Summer's body and get into her energy field without making the lost spirit aware of me. The energy of fear that the lost spirit attachment was feeding off of was weakened because Emma was distracted by the slight of hand tricks, and I was able to grab, and aggressively rip, the lost spirit out from Summer's body. In the past when I have done this, the lost spirit usually loses all its power and drops down pathetically weakened and disempowered, but not this one.

This lost spirit started to attack me, over and over again, projecting fierce energy towards me. I could also feel it trying to get back into Summer's energy field, I could feel it's intense anger and I could feel it's intention of getting back what it now believed, belonged to it, Summer. I focused on protecting Summer, I was 100% sure I was safe; I struggled to hold my focus as this lost spirit bounced so aggressively and irrationally around my healing room. I became frustrated with this lost spirit, and without thinking about it, I gathered my intention and forcefully pushed the lost spirit out past my window (and the wall of intent I have around my healing room that I use to hold a space only for the highest of good). As soon as the lost spirit was pushed out of my room and into the area outside of my window, the energetic space of the healing room quietened down. I was able to focus on securing Summer and sealing her aura; and allowing her natural protection to come back to full strength.

I looked outside to see if I could see the lost spirit, I wanted to know where it was as I worked on securing Summer, and also wanted to prepare myself to deal with and help this lost spirit. I was not going to just let it loose and allow it to become someone else's problem; what I saw was a first for me: The lost spirit was being wrapped in white energies. These energies were like nothing I had seen before or since. I cannot explain what they were, but it felt like they were attacking and capturing the lost spirit. I asked in my mind what was happening and the clear powerful reply I received was, *"what it was doing was unacceptable and we are taking him to the light against his will"*. Suddenly, like a shot, he was gone in a blur and the white energies outside my window were gone too.

I stayed with Summer's energy for a few minutes more. It was only 20 minutes since the start of the session, the lost spirit was gone, and Summer's energy field felt sealed and protected again. I know that children will always bounce back into their natural protection much more easily than adults; adults believe that it's possible for them to be spiritually unsafe, children don't think about these kinds of things. I explained what had happened to Emma. I was still playing with the purple pencil sharpener and decided to give it to Summer as a souvenir of her visit with me. Summer and Emma left and I felt quite exhausted.

*Cinematic movies and books represent spiritual attachments and spiritual possession as a negative, evil, and devilish type of experience. But to this day, I have never truly seen this, I have seen lost, hurt souls that are trapped on the earth plane, not knowing what to do to survive - doing things that are not acceptable. I have seen souls stuck in an understanding of the world from many years ago, not realising things have changed on the earth plane and that time has moved on, and most times they are easily removed. The experience with Summer was the most extreme I have so far encountered.*

*My first experience of spiritual possession was at 17 years old when I was doing my national service in the South African army. One of the recruits had become spiritually possessed and needed an exorcism. I witnessed him throwing six grown men off him as they tried to hold him down. These men were much larger than him yet it was a doddle for him to throw these huge, well trained, full-time army officers off his body. I also saw him lift an old television, you know those heavy things that need two people to carry them, and he easily lifted it above his head and tossed it at us like it was an empty cardboard box. He was exorcised in a church near our army base, and when we next saw him he looked weak and feeble for some time as his strength returned. I have no idea how and why he became possessed. But the experience is one I will never forget.*

*The first time I consciously did a depossession was in my healing room. A client was drawn to see me; she had been having a strange reaction in her body since she had been on holiday in Thailand and had been using recreational drugs.*

*This strange reaction of an uncontrollable retching only happened when she went into high energy areas like churches and spiritual groups, or whilst meditating. She had learned to stop the retching from happening to her by not going near these kinds of places, so she was mostly in control of her problem.*

*Her first session with me started normally, but within minutes she was retching with her head back almost constantly, with a really awful tearing type of sound coming from her throat and lungs. I do not believe it would be possible for someone to even consider faking those reactions or sounds, it was extreme. To say I was nervous is an understatement. I got her on the healing bed and opened myself to my guides for help. They told me to just hold the space for her and to see what would happen. Within a few moments this client started to literally bounce on the healing couch. My wooden portable healing couch was lifting off the floor as she bounced, making huge banging noises as the couch hit the floor. Loud guttural snarling noises were coming from her throat. My fear and uncertainty was at an extreme high at this time and obviously feeding this possession.*

*My guides stepped in to calm me and told me there was a man possessing her and that I must try to speak to him. Bravely I asked in my mind what he wanted. He showed himself to me, he was a dark skinned warrior. I asked why he was doing this to her. He told me she belonged to him. I asked why he thought she belonged to him. He said he was a tribal leader and he recognised her soul as that of a woman in his tribe, and that he owned her, she was his. At this point inspiration moved into my mind and I was not really in control of the process. I told him that he may think he owns her but she had control over him rather than him having control over her. She was his owner now because she could control when he got power by not going to high energy areas, like churches. I asked him how often he actually got control like he had right now. He went quiet. I said to him, "if you come out of her body I will send you to a place where you can be a tribal leader again." He thought and then instantly he was out of her body. He did not like the fact that she was actually in control of him. She sat bolt up-right and all the retching and bouncing stopped.*

*My client never had that same extreme retching again, and after having experienced a few weeks of habitual retching, it came to a complete stop. This tribal leader came to me later that day and I helped him off the earth plane into the light. He told me he did not realise the world had changed and he promised me his protection for helping him and the lady (my client). Many times since that day I have been told I have tribal warriors around me.*

*He was not an evil man, he was just trapped in a place*

*and state of mind, and with help, love and light, I was able to set him free and release a client from her problem. I have done hundreds of spirit removals or detachments. I have had to release little old ladies and children from clients. I have done removals in one to one sessions as well as in-front of groups. I have seen people's lives change almost instantly when this is done. In all the removals I have done, Summer's was the only one that I can say that the lost soul was doing something truly wrong or negative.*

*I recall clearing a little old lady from a 40-year old woman who was struggling with work and relationships in her life. When she lay on the bed all I could see was this little old lady. The little old lady told me that her name was Anya and that 20 years ago my client had been dropped whilst playing with a friend and was knocked out. Anya, a lost soul trapped between the earth and the spirit plane had stepped in to my client's energy when attempting to help her, but Anya got trapped in the client's body and did not know what to do to get out. My client confirmed that at 20 she had been dropped by a guy who had been flirting with her and was trying to show off. He had lifted her off the floor then lost control and dropped her on her head and knocked her out for a short time. My client could confirm that her life had never been the same after that day. After I removed Anya my client's life reverted, she found a new job and was engaged to be married within six months. Anya had been draining her power and slightly influencing all her decisions, not because Anya was negative, but because she was in an understanding of years past and had not realised the world was not like that anymore.*

## FEEDBACK

Over the next few days I started to get feedback from my friend and Emma. I was told that the morning after the session, Summer had told her mum that the horrible scary man was gone. No one had ever mentioned anything to Summer about her attachment. Emma told me that her zesty, vibrant daughter was back that very next morning, running about and being the same active child from before her initial illness. The doctors could not work out where the water around Summer's heart went. It was completely gone within 2 weeks. When I visited the restaurant the following week, Summer's dad approached me and said with a crackling emotional voice, "I do not understand or believe in the stuff that you do, but you brought my daughter back, thank you".

That same day, Emma told me that Summer would not

leave the house without the purple pencil sharpener, it had to go with her wherever she went. Summer had related her healing to the appearance and disappearance of the purple pencil sharpener. As I write this, I keep welling up with emotion. I am so thankful that I am able to help people but to help a child; well that is a true gift for me.

Thank you Summer.

*The last thing I was expecting was to find that Summer had associated the purple pencil sharpener as her rescuer and the thing that made her feel safe. Not only is it as cute as can be, but also a sign that, energetically, on a soul level, Summer was aware things were not going right for her, she had pushed her soul to the side to protect herself, and was obviously in some way aware of the man that was attacking her. The memory of that purple pencil sharpener will live with me forever.*

*Not everything that happens in our world is easily ex-plained. I have had to deal with things in my life that prob-ably make most people think I am a little bit 'out there' and have a few 'screws loose', and to be honest, I used to think the same way about myself. Even after doing an unexpected depossession on a member of a workshop that I was run-ning with 13 people watching and witnessing, the next day I was surprised and confused to get so many calls and emails telling me how amazing it was. Still in my mind, at that point, it was not real, it could not be real, even if 13 people had witnessed it.*

*It has taken me a long time to realise that this is real and these things do happen. When I asked Emma if I could write about her and Summer's experience with me, I was expecting an uncertain answer from Emma, but what I got was a complete and instant 'Yes!' and that Emma believes that clearing the spirit attachment from Summer saved her life. I am so often humbled by the things that happen in my career and life. I find even writing this book a little egotistical. All I can do is be honest and true in this book, I know nothing written here is anything but the truth, shared to the best of my abilities and memory. I constantly thank all my clients for choosing to allow me to help them.*

*I do not believe spirits can come to the earth plane and move things around and do things on our plane. I believe that they do not have the vibration or physical energetics to do that. But I do think they can manipulate the earth's energy to make things happen, so they need places or things that hold energy, such as lay-lines, or an old house or building. They can then gather the energy and push it with their intention. This will and focus of intention can allow them to do human activities in our thick, heavy gravity plane. This is why we get haunted houses and buildings, very seldom do you get haunting in a new building built on fresh ground.*

*Houses built on old building sites can also be haunted.*

*The other way spirits can get energy is from human be-ings, because we are on the earth and, as humans, we are born with an earth bound energetic, this is why our vibration is so much slower than that of spiritual souls. I allow my spirit doctors and guides to use energy from my body to work on clients; this is why on many occasions' people re-ceiving healing will feel more than just my pair of hands on their bodies. This is quite common with healers. In my work I have rules, I have set concepts that I have put in place that create for me specific situations of protection. For instance, as I have already said, I am always safe, no matter what my natural protection comes into place and works for me, always. Another is that wherever I work, I have a field of protection a good ten feet around the area I would be work-ing in. This field of protection is created to allow only spirit for the highest of good of the client to come in and help me with the session. Because of the thousands of times I have seen clients this field is powerful, and to my knowledge, has never been broken from the outside. Only this one time was it needed for me to push energetics out of this field. If I have an attachment or possession I will always deal with it in this space that I have created to keep the client and myself safe.*

## TESTIMONIAL

This is a testimonial from summers mother Emma.

By Summer's Mum - Emma Bovey

Wayne came into my family's life for a reason and that was to cure Summer. She has been seriously ill and in high intensity at the local hospital suffering from pneumonia and a large plural cavity around her heart.

What happened with Wayne was the most surreal experience that you could imagine; when you think of skies going black and a being chilled to the bone, well, you'd be in the right space! The lost soul I remember as being called Simon!

The result of our session was the all clear from the specialist at the hospital after 2 weeks, when the expectation was treatment for 6 months to 1 year.

Wayne I can't thank-you enough!

Go well Wayne,

Emma and Summer

# CONCLUSION

All I have, as a healer and a person, is my experiences. I am aware that every client brings new things for me to learn and I deeply appreciate it when a client finds me. I enjoy being there with my clients in their healing process. Lately it has become apparent that the universe wants me to spread my wings more and I believe this book is part of that process. A process of helping as many people as I possibly can.

Intuitive healing found me. It has given me the opportunity to find my personal path into self-development and inner trust. In a way it gave me the life I have now full of experiences and inspiration, I deeply love and appreciate the life I am leading.

I often get asked by my clients and friends; if when I walk down the street; am I able to see the same energetics as I do when I am working with a healing client, doing a psychic mediumship reading or running a spiritual workshop. The answer is yes, I can do, if I wanted to, but I do not. The reason I don't do this is that it is rude. It's like stopping strangers on the street and going through their pockets or hand bags, that would be rude and within no time the police would probably like to have a word with me about my behaviour.

So the answer is yes, I can read the energetics that is being projected of every person I come across or meet, I believe we all do this naturally we just need to learn to be aware of it more, but I choose when to allow my awareness to register with me for the sake of good manner and my own sanity.

One Tuesday evening after seeing clients in London, I was at London waterloo train station catching a train home and the station was as usual very busy, I had a half hour wait for my train and to use up some time I thought I would open myself up and see how it felt to connect in such a big and busy place. Wow! What a big mistake that was, it felt like I was in a war zone and loads of missiles where firing down at me with thousands of people screaming at me. I closed down very quickly. It was not scary or negative, just very busy and loud; I won't be doing that again in a hurry.

My work is important to me but I try and be, as much as possible in the human world we all live in, I profess that we should always be at least 51% human and never more than 49% in our spirituality because we are humans on an earth plane. So I try and live my life as much as I can, to the fullest I can, although I am really good at and enjoy being still and quiet.

I hope this book inspires people to trust themselves and

to be opened to their personal outrageous outgoing concepts, no matter if they are right or wrong, as long as intention is for the highest of good and the outcome has helped them or someone else to grow.

I trust that this book will bring love into people lives and helps them be more themselves.

If one person is inspired to seek help or gains self-understanding from this book it will be a success to me.

Thank you, I love you, please forgive me, I am sorry, I love you.

Printed in the USA
CPSIA information can be obtained
at www.ICGtesting.com
LVHW010130150324
774508LV00002B/286

9 781999 963026